TAIJIQUAN In 88 Forms

Compiled by Victor Wu
Translated by Huang Jun

(Revised Edition)

HAI FENG PUBLISHING COMPANY
HONG KONG

First Edition 1983

Published by
Hai Feng Publishing Co., Ltd.
Rm. 1503 Wing On House,
71 Des Voeux Rd. C., Hong Kong.

Printed by
Friendly Printing Co., Ltd.
Flat B1, 3/F., Luen Ming Hing Ind. Bldg.,
36 Muk Cheong Street, Tokwawan,
Kowloon, H.K.

Distributed by
China International Book Trading Corporation
(GUOJI SHUDIAN)
P.O. Box 399, Beijing, China

Printed in Hong Kong

太極拳八十八式

中華人民共和國
體育運動委員會 編

海峰出版社有限公司出版
(香港德輔道中71號永安集團大廈1503室)

友利印刷有限公司印刷
(香港九龍土瓜灣木廠街36號4樓B1座)

中國國際圖書貿易總公司發行
(中國國際書店)
北京399信箱

1988年（報紙本）第一版
編號：（英文版）

ISBN 962-238-049-2
HF-57-P
T-E-1902P

ACKNOWLEDGEMENTS

This is a translation of the authentic "Taijiquan Exercises" published in China, of which 1,512,000 copies have been sold. To translate such a traditional Chinese concept into English is quite a challenge to oneself, because it requires not only the mastery of the two languages but also a correct interpretation of its subtleties through personal experience of the exercises.

The present work is done with literal fidelity to the Chinese original by a translator, himself a practitioner for three years. He is deeply indebted to Prof. Wang Zhong-yan, Ms. Moya Brenum, Prof. William de Mille, and Mrs. Rosina Simonelli Singer in America for their kind advice and suggestions that have helped to improve this work.

Huang Jun
Jinan University, Guangzhou
October, 1980

CONTENTS

Chapter One
Introduction — 1

   I. Why Taijiquan is Good for Your Health — 2
   II. The Main Features, Basic Rules and Positions of the Body — 9
   III. Three Stages for Practice — 21

Chapter Two
Taijiquan — Its 88 Forms — 25

   I. List of Forms — 26
   II. Instruction on Techniques — 29
   III. The Diagram of Footwork for Taijiquan (88-Forms) — 184

Chapter Three
The Taiji Push-Hands — 187

   I. Basic Training — 189
   II. Stationary Push-Hands — 203
   III. Mobile Push-Hands — 210

Chapter One
INTRODUCTION

I. Why Taijiquan is Good for Your Health

Taijiquan is a traditional Chinese art in physical culture, and has been very popular among the people since ancient days. Centuries of practice have testified to its value in preservation of health and prevention of diseases. Now as part of physical exercise therapy in clinical practice, it has been widely reported to be not only health-preserving but actually beneficial to patients with high blood pressure, stomach or intestinal ulcers, heart troubles, tuberculosis and other ailments. In fact, China has been one of the first to apply physical exercise in therapy and health preservation. Our oldest medical classic, *Huang Di's Medical Textbook: A Dialogue,* says, "Those who are constantly ill, fatigued or assailed by fever should be treated with conducive methods." (Here, "Conducive methods" means light physical exercises.) Later, our ancient medical scientists went on to expound how such methods worked. More than 1,800 years ago, the preeminent Dr Hua Tuo devised a "Five-animal Play", a set of physical exercise based on the theory that "a constantly active body is free from indigestion, circulatory trouble and other physical problems, just like the door-hinge which is free from rot or rust." All this clearly illustrates the importance of physical culture in therapy and disease prevention.

In practising Taijiquan, not only are all the muscles and joints in motion, but breathing and movement of the diaphragm must be regulated to the tempo, and the practitioner is required to remain "calm" yet fully concentrated. This will produce a unique sedative effect upon the central nervous system, which in turn helps activate or improve the functions of other bodily systems.

To verify this effect, Beijing Sports Medical Research Centre carried out an investigation among the aged, ranging from 50 to 89. Of these, 32 regularly practised Taijiquan as contrasted with 56 others who did not. The comparison revealed that the former were categorically stronger than the latter, not only in general physical condition, but also in functions of metabolism and the cardio-vascular, respiratory and skeletal systems.

Following is the analysis of the physiological effect of Taijiquan on each main system of the human body.

A. What Taijiquan is able to do for the Nervous System

From latest developments in physiology, particularly through the studies of the central nervous system, we realize more and more the important role it plays in the human body. We know that the nervous system, especially the brain, is the centre that governs and regulates all other systems and organs. Through the functioning of the nervous system (both conditioned and unconditioned reflexes), man adapts to his environment and transforms it. At the same time, he readjusts the activities of all bodily systems and organs. Therefore any physical exercise that improves the function of the central nervous system is beneficial for the whole body. So is Taijiquan.

In practising Taijiquan, one is required to be "Calm", fully concentrated and able to direct full attention to any part of his body, which is in itself very good discipline for the mind. Besides, in action, he has to move his eyes, upper limbs, torso and lower limbs smoothly without discord or abrupt stops. And owing to the complexity of some movements, he must have a good control of his body and sense of balance, which can only be achieved by intense activity of the brain and thus fully mobilizes the central nervous system as well as all other systems and organs.

Indeed, Taijiquan is a highly absorbing sport. All practitioners share a unique experience: complete relaxation and a radiant glow in solo; unexpected agility and quick response in duet. Such are eloquent signs of a buoyant mood and high motivation, which enliven the physiological mechanism of the whole body. Experiments prove that even before the exertion in action, one's mood alone may affect the chemical content of the blood, dynamic process of circulation, gaseous metabolism etc. To patients of chronic diseases, a buoyant mood is all the more important, as it not only activates all manners of physiological mechanism, but helps to eliminate the patient's morbid mentality, and is conducive to recuperation.

The above testifies to a positive effect of Taijiquan upon the central nervous system.

B. What Taijiquan is able to do for the Cardiovascular and Respiratory Systems

The effect of the exercise upon the cardiovascular system is determined by the practitioner's nervous system. The movements of Taijiquan activate the muscles and joints, produce rhythmic breathing especially involving the diaphragm. Therefore it spurs the blood and lymph circulation and reduces Ecchymosis (escape of blood into the tissues from ruptured blood vessels), and is indeed a good way to eliminate such an ailment.

As we all know, the regular contraction and expansion of all the skeletal muscles help blood circulation in the veins and ensure the return of the veinous blood as well as the necessary vascular pressure in the right auricle of the heart. Regular breathing is also an aid to the circulation, for, as the volume of the chest increases at inhalation, the internal negative pressure rises, which in turn decreases the pressure in the vena cava sup and inf (two large veins carrying blood to the heart), speeding up the return of the veinous blood.

With the chest relaxed, Taijiquan movements are smooth and well adjusted to the tempo of breathing to make it natural, giving full play to its total effect and further improving the blood and lymph circulation. Very often, when an athlete's chest, shoulder and elbow muscles are strained under exertion, his breathing is apparently handicapped by a constrained chest, which results in the obstruction of blood circulation, a flushed face, and bulging veins in the neck. Taijiquan practitioners never show such symptons.

Many movements of the exercise require a kind of "Abdominal restraint", which is a special form of diaphragmatic breathing very good for the practitioner's health. The regular workings of the diaphragm and abdominal muscles keep the abdominal pressure fluctuating. As the rising pressure reaches the veins, blood is pumped into the right auricle; conversely, when the pressure falls, blood is pumped back into the abdomen. Thus the rhythmic breathing of the exercise improves blood circulation and nourishment of the cardiac muscles. What is more, the diaphragmatic movements can also provide a constant massage for the liver, and this is indeed a good way to clear up hepatic ecchymosis (stagnant blood in the liver) and improve the liver's function. Therefore, regular exercise is a good antidote to many kinds of heart trouble and arteriosclerosis.

According to the report of a test conducted by Beijing Sports Medicine Research Centre between the two aged groups mentioned before, both stepping up and down a bench 40 cm high 15 times, Group A was superior in cardiovascular function. All but one of the 32 completed the quota with normal blood pressure and pulse. Meanwhile, in Group B, the control group, the higher the age was, the poorer the performance, with poor reaction recorded, such as, the type and over weight types and were total failures. Cardiographs confirmed the tests. In Group A, 28.2% of the cases were abnormal, whereas in Group B, there were 41.3% abnormal. The statistics illustrate that regular practice ensures sufficient supply of blood to the coronary artery, a powerful heart contraction and a smooth dynamic process of blood circulation.

Not only that, but as constant practice of Taijiquan improves the governing power of the central nervous system and coordination among the organs, and increases the intensity of the vagus nerve, the supply of blood and oxygen and the process of metabolism are all stepped up. Naturally, fewer cases of high blood pressure and arteriosclerosis were found among Group A, in which the average blood pressure was 134.1/80.8 mm Hg as compared to 154.5/82.7 mm Hg of the other. The rate of arteriosclerosis in Group A was 39.5% while the general average for people of that age is 46.4%.

Physical examinations prove that Taijiquan exercises are beneficial in preserving lung elasticity, chest activity (preventing hardening of the rib cartilage), lung ventilation capacity and metabolic exchange of oxygen and carbon dioxide. Group A's breathing capacity was much higher than Group B's, which points clearly to the greater power of the respiratory and diaphragm muscles, higher lung elasticity and lower rate of hardening of the rib cartilage in the former group. To those already suffering from hardening of the rib cartilage and obstruction in chest activity, the deep and slow breathing and abdominal muscle movement during practice not only increases ventilation activities, but through the rhythmic fluctuation of abdominal pressure, speeds up the blood stream and gaseous exchange in the lung cells, and helps preserve the patient's vitality. That is why the members of Group A were able to maintain an even breath and make a quick recovery after their test.

C. *What the exercise is able to do for the Skeleton, Muscles and Joints*

Taijiquan does a lot of good to the skeleton, muscles and joints of the body. Take the spinal column for instance, the practitioner must keep his "chest in, waist and back relaxed", and let his spinal column at the waist section be "the primary axis of movement". This clealy shows how much all the movements are centered around the waist. Regular practice will no doubt maintain a good spinal column position and organic structure. By observation in Group A, there were only 25.8% cases of spinal deformity, whereas the general average for that age group is 47.2%. Although the hunch back is a typical deformity of the aged, much fewer of such cases are found among the regular practitioners. Besides, the extent of the practitioner's spinal activity is larger too. 77.4% in Group A could bend and touch the ground, while only 16.6% of the other group could do the same. X-ray pictures revealed that the rate of old age osteomalacia (softening of the bones) was also much lower in Group A (36.6% as against 63.8%). We know that the main cause of such cases lies in the inactivity of boney cells and deficiency of the ossein, which leads to deformity and immobility. The Taijiquan movements are all smoothly linked together, mobilizing every joint, which is deterent to ageing.

D. What the exercise is able to do for the Metabolism of Bodily Substance

Not much information is available so far in this area. Yet from the differences in skeletal change and rate of arteriosclerosis between the two groups, it is obvious that the exercise does a lot of good to the metabolism of lipid, protein and inorganic salts, such as calcium and phosphorous. Recently extensive studies have been made in the world on the de-ageing effect of sports from the approach of substantial metabolism. For example, it has been reported that the cholesterol content in an aged patient's blood will decrease after exercise from 5 to 30 minutes, particularly so with those who have a high cholestrol content in blood. Studies have also been made on the metabolism of aged arteriosclerosis patients before and after exercise. It was shown that their albumin content in blood had increased, while the contents of globulin and cholesterol had obviously decreased, with the symptons of arteriosclerosis greatly alleviated. These results fully indicate the positive effect of Taijiquan on the metabolism of bodily substance.

E. *What the exercise is able to do for the Digestive System*

As mentioned above, since improvement of the nerve system will better mobilize all other systems, the exercise will prevent and even cure illnesses of the digestive system in motion, secretion and assimilation, which arise from nervous functional disorders. Besides, the respiratory movement can be a mechanistic stimulant to the gastro-intestinal tracts, quicken the blood circulation and thereby improve digestion and prevent constipation — all of which are essential to the aged.

To sum up, Taijiquan is a gentle sport well suited to the laws of physiology.

II. The Main Features, Basic Rules and Positions of the Body

A. The Main Features

1. *Mildness and Gentleness* The basic stance is steady and unstrained, and the movements should be smooth and gentle, without Sunday punches or vigorous leaps. That is why after practising the whole set once or twice, there is hardly any panting, but only a light perspiration over the whole body and a sense of satisfaction. For this reason alone, Taijiquan is almost suited to anybody, regardless of age, sex or physique. It is an excellent therapeutic exercise, particularly for the feeble and the chronically diseased.

2. *Continuity and Evenness* From beginning to end, all the movements, including shifting of weight and moving from one position to another, are closely linked in an endless chain without a break. They follow one another at an even and unhurried pace like floating clouds or a smooth running stream.

3. *Natural and Circular Movement* The style of Taijiquan distinguishes itself from others by its unique circular movements of the upper limbs, avoiding direct and straight impact, which is in conformity with the natural curvature of bodily joints. The exercise helps shape one's movements into gentle curves with a natural grace.

4. *Concord and Consistency* Throughout the exercise, with every single movement or position, the practitioner's upper half and lower half, "Inner self" (attention and breath) and "outer self" (the torso and limbs) must be at one. In fact, there must be perfect coordination of the whole body, with the waist as the main axis. Even the hands and feet have to follow the body without any discord.

Such are the artistic features of Taijiquan.

B. Basic Rules

1. *The Mind Directs All The Movements* Except for the reflexes, all human actions, including those in sports training, must be directed by the mind. Likewise, in practising Taijiquan, the mind (particularly its power of imagery) is dominant, directing the practitioner's attention completely to his action throughout the whole process. For instance, at the "Opening Form" when both arms are gently raised, like the "arm front horizontal raise" in callisthenics, the practitioner must first picture the action before he actually does so. Or, in pushing out, he must see the image in his mind before he pushes out his hands. When he intends to hold down his "qi" (breath or center of attention), there must be a vision of something going down to the depths of his abdomen. As the stream of his consciousness runs on, so do his actions, threaded *as it were* on a string. In fact, throughout the exercise, from "Opening Form" till "Closing Form", all actions are directed by the mind, or rather, mental images. As the saying goes, "The mind is the master, the body its servant", or "The body follows the mind." Therefore, the following must be observed:

   a) *Calm* From the very beginning, the practitioner must be perfectly calm, with nothing on his mind, except making sure that his head is erect, his body and arms relaxed and his breath smooth. He is not to start unless he is sure of all these. This is most essential before *practice begins.* And the serenity of mind must last throughout the whole exercise, whether the action is simple or complicated, the stance high or low. Only in this way can his mind be fully concentrated and guide every minute detail of his action, otherwise he is bound to be in disharmony. Taijiquan requires "calmness through action" and "action under calmness". Thus, there will be no excessive mental strain or fatigue in practice.

b) *Full Concentration* Apart from being calm, the practitioner must direct his attention to his actions and see that every movement conforms to the basic rules throughout the exercise. He must never allow his eyes or mind to wander during practice. However, beginners often neglect this rule of "Concentration". This can be overcome through practice, which will make the actions follow the mind naturally, and when the two are in perfect harmony, strength will grow.

2. *Relax; No Hard Force* "Relax" here does not mean complete slackness, but a loosening of certain muscles and joints and ease of movement without using hard, inflexible strength. The correct stance is to hold the spine naturally erect, so that the head, body and limbs can all move with ease. Do not lean forward, backward or sideways; just maintain a correct and steady posture with what is called "well regulated strength" or "internal force". When your arms are to be rounded, keep them fully rounded; when your leg is to be bent, bend it as required, and with the right amount of strength while all other muscles are relaxed. Beginners naturally will find it difficult to keep within the limits. They should however, first learn to

relax, with all the joints unhampered by strain so as to keep their muscles flexible. From "relaxation", they will gradually learn to muster strength, and keep moving continuously with fluidity and perfect harmony.

3. *Coordinate Upper and Lower Half To Achieve Harmony*
Taijiquan is an overall physical training. It is often so described: "A single movement sets the whole body moving" and "Action goes on from foot to leg and then to body in complete harmoney." This illustrates the meaning of the word "coordination".

Theoretically, beginners may know well that the lumbar spine is the axis of most actions, and that the limbs should follow the movement of body, yet owing to discord between mind and body, it is often difficult for them to achieve complete coordination or harmony in action. Therefore, it is better to start with practice of separate "forms", such as, the "Opening Form", "Wave Hands Like Moving Clouds" etc, in order to coordinate body and limbs. They should also practise certain steps in footwork, such as, the "hollow step", "bow step" and shifting of weight and footsteps to strengthen the supporting lower limbs and master the rudiments of footwork. Then they can go on to combine the two into one through the whole series and gradually master the art of coordination so as to give their body a thorough training and a balanced development.

4. *Master "Hollow-Solid" Transformation To Keep Balance* On learning the basic movements and coordination, the learner should direct his attention to the "hollow-solid" transformation and shifting of weight centre, which go through every movement and step of the exercise. He should also pay attention to the movement of his body and hands, turning them from "hollow" to "solid" or vice versa, in definite contrast and without pause, so that his stream of

consciousness flows on in spite of variation in movement from beginning to end. If he fails to master the subtle transformation, his footwork will surely flounder, causing sluggish movement or instability. The saying, "The gait of a cat, the strength of a silkworm", aptly describes the deftness in footwork and evenness of strength in movement of Taijiquan. The key to it is precision in "hollow-solid" transformation, which keeps body and limbs well balanced in motion. Failing this, there can be no deftness and evenness in strength at all. (cf. "Hollow-solid" transformation in the coming passage "Basic Positions")

However complex the movement may be, the learner should first of all keep himself unhurried and unstrained, which is the fundamental requirement of Taijiquan, called "central gravity". Before turning, always keep body balanced first; while moving ahead or back always set the lifted foot on ground before shifting weight gradually. Meanwhile, the lowered shoulders, relaxed waist and hips as well as the "hollow-solid" movement of hands all add to stability. Thus trained through constant practice, the learner will never lose his balance whether he moves swiftly or slowly.

5. *Breathe Naturally* Taijiquan requires the practitioner's breath to be natural, free from panting. Indeed, in any kind of sports activity, the oxygen required by the human body far exceeds what one needs in a static condition. Yet in practising Taijiquan, owing to the gentleness of movement, the body goes through a harmonious adjustment, which can supply all the oxygen needed by deep breathing without much effort.

Beginners should first of all learn to keep their breath natural, i.e., breathe as they normally do, without trying to adjust their breath to the movement of the exercise.

When they get more skilled, they can adjust it merely

by their own awareness to the pace and stretch of their own movements in the manner of up-inhale; down-exhale, open-inhale; close-exhale, uniting breath and movement in one. For instance, while lifting the arms gradually in the Opening Form, they should inhale, and while, bending knees and lowering arms, exhale. The breathing should accompany the rise and fall of the chest cavity and the diaphragm, according to the needs of movement and body to increase the activity of diaphragm and the supply of oxygen. However, in movements without apparent rise and fall or open and close, or with people working at different pace, the coordination of movement and breath must not be arbitrary. Otherwise there will be more harm than good, resulting in laboured breath or discord in movement.

The above are by no means separate independent rules but interdependent elements. Without calmness, one can not concentrate, which makes it impossible to keep body and mind at one, not to speak of continuity and flexibility in motion. Without "hollow-solid" transformation or control of weight, the torso will be strained, making it impossible to coordinate and integrate the movements, and there can be no natural breathing.

C. Basic Positions

1. *The Head* In practice, the position of the head must be strictly maintained. The description, "Head erect, with neck relaxed" stipulates that the practitioner should hold his head upright without straining neck muscles or allowing it to sway. The movement of neck must coordinate with the change in position of body and turning of torso. The facial expression should be natural, chin drawn in and mouth either left open or closed with tip of tongue on

palate to not draw saliva.

With the turn of body, the eyes should either rest upon the hand in front (in a few cases, upon the hand in in rear) or look straight ahead without closing or staring in any angry glare. While practising, one must look fully composed yet concentrated to achieve the best effects.

2. *The Body*
   a) *Chest and Back* One of the basic rules is "Keep chest in and back relaxed" or "Restrain the chest, move only shoulders", i.e., while practising, do not throw out the chest, nor keep it too far in, but just be natural. In fact, "chest in" and "back relaxed" are correlated, which allows the spinal muscles to stretch freely as arms extend in motion. Meanwhile, see that the muscles on chest are relaxed to eliminate tension on ribs and thus ensure natural breathing.
   b) *Spine* The spine is the kingpin of human body in various positions as standing, walking, sitting, and lying. So in practising Taijiquan, the spine plays a most important role in keeping body erect and at ease. That is why people say, "The spine is the mainstay", "Heed the lumbar section every minute but with abdomen relaxed, and you will feel strength growing quickly," and "The lumbar spine is the axis", which means that without the lumbar section as axis or central switch of strength, the movement of the whole body will be in discord. While in practice, whether going forward or backward, or turning, or changing from "hollow" to "solid" in movement, keep the waist relaxed so as to conduct *"qi"* downward. Do not thrust out the belly to ensure freedom in turning or change of position. Besides, the relaxation of the waist will also strengthen the legs, reinforcing the basis of

the posture to allow flexibility and integration of movement.

Remember: In keeping the waist section relaxed, the spine must be held normally erect, neither crouching nor jutting out the lower backbone, nor inclined to either side to avoid unnecessary strain on the chest or belly. With the weight of body supported by the waist, all the movements will become steady and free. From this you can see the spine is the "mainstay" in practising Taijiquan.

c) *The Hips* They should be held "in". Avoid jutting them out and spoiling the natural position, or twisting sideways. With the waist relaxed and spine erect, hold the body straight. But like the head, the hips should be kept in position by mental awareness rather than by strength.

3. *The Legs* They determine the direction in movement, provide the source of strength, and ensure stability of body. Therefore, in practice, special care is given to the shifting of weight, the position of either foot and the bending of legs. The practitioners often say, "The strength is rooted in the feet, gathered in legs, centered in the waist and shown in the fingers." From this we can see how important the movement and position of the legs are to the stance of the whole body.

In moving the legs, the joints of hips and knees should be kept free to allow swift movement forward or backward. The lifting and lowering of foot should be light and deft; when going forward, rest heel first on ground, when going backward, put the ball of foot down before the entire foot is gradually set firm.

Beginners often find it hard to divide their attention

between hands and feet, and most of them can only take care of their upper limbs, neglecting footwork to the detriment of the basic stance. So due attention should be given to changing position in footwork until it is fully mastered. In "setting the frame", or, basic training, they must learn to appreciate the subtle "hollow-solid" transformation, and avoid resting their weight on both legs except in "Opening Form", "Closing Form" and "Close Hand". The technique is simply a matter of shifting weight from one leg to another. When it rests on right leg, the right one is "solid" and the left is "hollow", and vice versa. Nevertheless, the "hollow" foot is still a support to keep body balanced, such as, the fore foot in a "hollow step", or the rear foot in a "bow step". Therefore the transformation must be clear-cut, but not carried to extremes, as the legs must be able to move steadily with ease and take rest by turns to lessen fatigue.

In a bow step, the bent leg supports the weight while the other is slightly raised and stretched (but not taut), resting naturally first on the heel, then gradually on the entire sole, and pushing ahead. In this way the practitioner can move forward or backward with ease, at a natural pace. In a follow-up step, the sole must first rest on ground, while the kick and separation of feet must go slow (with very few exceptions) in order to keep the body well balanced. Sweeping the ground or slapping the foot should never be strained; the practitioner need not touch his foot at all in "Slapping" it, if it does not suit him.

4. *The Arms* "Shoulders lowered and elbows loose" is a Taijiquan jargon meaning that the joints of these parts should be relaxed. In fact, the joints of shoulder and elbow are closely connected. When shoulders are lowered, elbows are naturally loose. In practice, keep both shoulder joints

relaxed, lowered and consciously extended.

The hand position is: when drawn, the palm should be slightly cupped but not softened nor buoyant; while pushing, not only lower shoulder and loosen elbow, but keep wrist down a little without being rigid. When it bends, extends or turns, the hand should move with a light deftness. While extending the palm, the fingers should be well stretched out but slightly bent. Never clench the fist too tight.

The movement of hand should be in line with that of shoulder. If it goes too far forward, the arm will be fully straightened, which is against the rule "shoulders lowered and elbows loose". Yet if shoulders are too much lowered and elbows over-loosened, the out-going hand will be neglected, resulting in a crooked arm. After all, in motion, the arms must be well rounded, and the hands should never push out or withdraw abruptly, so that the movements will be well controlled and continued, light but not buoyant, steady but not rigid, and gracefully flexible.

D. Points for Attention (A Few Tips)

1. *An Even Pace* Beginners should go slow rather than fast in practice. Laying a solid foundation through slow motion, they should first learn to master the movements as well as the basic rules. When they become more skillful, they should keep at an even pace, whether fast or slow, throughout the exercise. Normally, the "Simplified Taijiquan" lasts about 4-6 minutes. At a slower pace, it may be lengthened to 8 or 9 minutes, but not much more. The complete series of "88-Form Taijiquan" takes about 20 minutes.

2. *A Steady Stance* Beginners may practise with a basic stance high or low, but they should set a definite height at "Open-

ing Form", and keep to it throughout the whole series (with the exception of "Low Form"). Weak practitioners should preferably stay high, and gradually come down to mid-high or low as they become more skillful and fit.

3. *A Proper Work-Out Load* Although Taijiquan is not so tough-going as callisthenics or other kinds of martial arts, it requires the lower limbs to move bent in slow motion, and in full concentration and coordination of the whole body. Therefore, it means a considerable work-load, especially for lower limbs. Owing to frequent "hollow-solid" transformation, weight is often shifted to one single leg, usually bent; also, moving from one form to another is deliberately kept slow, adding much to the load on lower limbs. That is why beginners, on practising "Simplified Taijiquan" once or twice, will often feel aching in the legs, and this is perfectly normal. They should persist with the exercise and the aching will soon vanish. The work-out program each time, i.e., duration, frequency and load, should be based on one's working (or schooling) and physical conditions. Those who are healthy can naturally take a heavier load by practising the whole series once or twice, The old and feeble should adjust their program according to their own condition by practising only one or several series, or merely one or two forms, such as "'Grasp the Peacock's Tail", "Wave Hands like Moving Clouds", "Opening Form" etc, or at a higher stance. For instance, in a "bow step", the knee should be vertical to the toes, but in the present case, the angle at the knee can be widened. For patients, the load should first be reduced and gradually stepped up, with the doctor's approval if necessary. In a word, at the beginning, the load should be controlled according to each person's condition and not be made too heavy.

4. *Perseverence* As in other sports, "perseverence" is the watch-word for Taijiquan practitioners. Do not give up when your health begins to improve. It is such a wondrous exercise that it not only prevents but actually cures diseases. Every day before or after work, or at daybreak go to a quiet corner or any patch of open ground and practise. The effect is even better if you can do it early at dawn or late at night in a park, wood, square or by the side of a river or a sea where the air is fresh and tranquil. If there is a group, so much the better. You will not only improve your performance but have a deeper grasp of the rules through discussion and exchanging tips.

III. Three Stages for Practice

A. Stage One

In Stage One the training items are the basic forms (at completion) and movements (in transition), i.e., master the rudiments: the steps, footwork, leg movements, body positions, forms of hand, hand movements and direction of eyes. All these must be correct, steady, gentle and performed with ease.

B. Stage Two

The focus of attention in this stage is on the transition from one movement to another and the basic rules until the movements are well connected and coordinated, curved and flexible, and cultivated with a natural grace.

C. Stage Three

It is said that practising Taijiquan is a process of acquisition "from skill to appreciation". "Appreciation" here means insights into the movements and mastering transmission of strength.

In the past, indeed, there were interpretations of Taijiquan that tended to mystify rather than clarify the meaning of its movements and training process. Following are the targets for training in the final stage, and perhaps, a few words of explanation are necessary:

1. *"Hollow-Solid" Well Defined; Hardness and Softness Inter-*

mingled Every Taijiquan movement embodies a process of unification of opposites. Often one leg or hand "hollow", the other "solid", and the roles are exchanged. And at the end of a movement, the joints and muscles should be left flexible for action, and this is called "solidity in hollowness, hollowness in solidity". This means that exertion should be kept within limits: Although it is aimed at the main target, minor (other possible) targets are not overlooked, and there is hardness in softness of movement and softness in hardness to avoid either stiffness or flaccidiness. Every movement at any moment contains mutually accomodating opposing forces, and proceeds through their contention and mutual complementation.

2. *Continuity and Unity of Strength* Here continuity and unity mean that strength must run on, shifting from one part of body to another without any break, while the whole body, with the waist as the pivot, is well coordinated in movement (re. II.A. The Main Features b,d)

   The greatest variety of movement lies in the arms, which fully demonstrate the incessant flow of strength. For instance, when the arm moves out or in, the forearm would turn slightly outward or in with attention on the middle finger or the thumb. This allows variation to occur with fluid, continued and unified strength.

3. *Concentration and Presence of Mind over Action* Beginners' minds are mostly occupied by "What comes next in action?" of "Am I doing it right?" As they get on, they will turn their attention to the application or transmission of strength, guiding it conscienciously with their minds, which are alive with imagination. (re. II.B. Basic Rules a,) However they should note:

   a) Full concentration does not mean dull and pointless

mental strain.
b) Practice should be an enjoyable experience.
c) The mind, strength and movement are one, and in that order.

4. *Breathing Naturally Adjusted to Movement* The rule given in II.B. Basic Rules e, should not be misinterpreted. It is to be applied only where movements up and down or open and close are apparent. One should not simply make an arbitrary "Inhale-Exhale Program" and work on it throughout the whole exercise, as this will do more harm than good.

Chapter Two

TAIJIQUAN — ITS 88 FORMS

I. List of Forms

Form 1	Pre-Opening Stance	預備式
Form 2	Opening Form	起勢
Form 3	Grasp Peacock's Tail	攬雀尾
Form 4	Single Whip	單鞭
Form 5	Raise Hands	提手
Form 6	White Crane Spreading Wings	白鶴亮翅
Form 7	Brush Knee & Twist Step — Left	左摟膝拗步
Form 8	Hands Strumming the Lute	手揮琵琶
Form 9	Brush Knee & Twist Step — Left & Right	左右摟膝拗步
Form 10	Hands Strumming the Lute	手揮琵琶
Form 11	Step Up, Parry & Punch	進步搬攔捶
Form 12	Apparent Close-Up	如封似閉
Form 13	Cross Hands	十字手
Form 14	Return to Mountain with Tiger	抱虎歸山
Form 15	Obliquely Grasp Peacock's Tail	斜攬雀尾
Form 16	First under Elbow	肘底看捶
Form 17	Slip Back Foream — Left & Right	左右倒卷肱
Form 18	Oblique Flying	斜飛式
Form 19	Raise Hands	提手
Form 20	White Crane Spreading Wings	白鶴亮翅
Form 21	Brush Knee & Twist Step	左摟膝拗步
Form 22	Needle at Sea Bottom	海底針
Form 23	Flash Out Arms	閃通臂
Form 24	Turn, Sidle & Punch	轉身撇身捶
Form 25	Step Up, Parry & Punch	進步搬攔捶
Form 26	Step Up & Grasp Peacock's Tail	上步攬雀尾

Form 27	Single Whip	單鞭
Form 28	Wave Hands Like Clouds	雲手
Form 29	Single Whip	單鞭
Form 30	High Pat on Horse	高探馬
Form 31	Right Kick	右分脚
Form 32	Left Kick	左分脚
Form 33	Turn & Left Kick	轉身左蹬脚
Form 34	Brush Knee & Twist Step	左右摟膝拗步
Form 35	Step Up & Punch Down	進步栽捶
Form 36	White Snake Showing Tongue	翻身白蛇吐信
Form 37	Step Up, Parry & Punch	進步搬攔捶
Form 38	Kick with Right Heel	右蹬脚
Form 39	Siddle Left to Tame Tiger	左披身伏虎
Form 40	Sidle Right to Tame Tiger	右披身伏虎
Form 41	About-Turn & Kick with Right Heel	回身右蹬脚
Form 42	Strike Opponent's Ears with Both Fists	雙峯貫耳
Form 43	Kick with Left Heel	左蹬脚
Form 44	Turn & Kick with Right Heel	轉身右蹬脚
Form 45	Step up, Parry & Punch	進步搬攔捶
Form 46	Apparent Close-Up	如封似閉
Form 47	Cross Hands	十字手
Form 48	Return to Mountain with Tiger	抱虎歸山
Form 49	Obliquely Grasp Peacock's Tail	斜攬雀尾
Form 50	Side-Step Single Whip	橫單鞭
Form 51	Parting Wild Horse's Mane — Left & Right	左右野馬分鬃
Form 52	Step Up & Grasp Peacock's Tail	進步攬雀尾
Form 53	Single Whip	單鞭
Form 54	Working at Shuttles (at 4 Angles)	左右穿梭（四斜角）
Form 55	Step Up & Grasp Peacock's Tail	進步攬雀尾
Form 56	Single Whip	單鞭
Form 57	Wave Hands Like Moving Clouds	雲手
Form 58	Single Whip	單鞭
Form 59	Sweep Down	下勢

Form 60	Golden Cock on One Leg
	— Left & Right 左右金鷄獨立
Form 61	Slip Back Arm — Left & Right 左右倒卷肱
Form 62	Oblique Flying 斜飛式
Form 63	Raise Hands 提手
Form 64	White Crane Spreading Wings 白鶴亮翅
Form 65	Brush Knee & Twist Step — Left 左摟膝拗步
Form 66	Needle at Sea Bottom 海底針
Form 67	Flash Out Arms 閃通臂
Form 68	Turn, Sidle & Punch 轉身撇身捶
Form 69	Step Up, Parry & Punch 進步搬攔捶
Form 70	Step Up & Grasp Peacock's Tail 上步攬雀尾
Form 71	Single Whip 單鞭
Form 72	Wave Hands Like Moving Clouds 雲手
Form 73	Single Whip 單鞭
Form 74	High Pat on Horse 高探馬
Form 75	Cross Palms (Back to Back) — Left 左穿掌
Form 76	Turn, Cross Hands & Kick 轉身十字蹬腳
Form 77	Brush Knee & Punch 摟膝打捶
Form 78	Step Up & Grasp Peacock's Tail 上步攬雀尾
Form 79	Single Whip 單鞭
Form 80	Sweep Down 下勢
Form 81	Step Up to Form Seven Stars 上步七星
Form 82	Retreat to Mount Tiger 退步跨虎
Form 83	Turn & Swing up Lotus-Leg 轉身擺蓮脚
Form 84	Archer Shooting Tiger 彎弓射虎
Form 85	Step Up, Parry & Punch 進步搬攔捶
Form 86	Apparent Close-Up 如封似閉
Form 87	Cross Hands 十字手
Form 88	Closing Form 收勢還原

II. Instruction on Techniques

1 2

Form 1 Pre-Opening Stance

Body stands naturally erect with feet shoulder-width apart, toes pointing forward. Arms hang loose with hands on sides of thighs. Eyes front. (Figs. 1, 2)

Remember:

> Neck is straight with chin in. Do not thrust out chest or draw in abdomen. Be fully concentrated.

3   4

Form 2   Opening Form

1) Both arms are gradually raised horizontal, hands at shoulder level and shoulder-width apart, palms downward. (Fig. 3)

   Remember:
   In raising arms, the movement must be slow and light as feather without strain.

2) Both knees bend and palms depress with elbows hung in position in correspondence with knees. Eyes front. (Fig. 4)

   Remember:
   Shoulders are lowered and elbows hung loose with fingers slightly crooked. Knees are bent, waist section relaxed and buttocks drawn in with weight on both legs. Lowering of arms should be coordinated with crouching of body.

5   6

Form 3 Grasp Peacock's Tail

1) With right toes slightly turning out, body turns right a little, and right arm is bent horizontally before chest while left hand draws an arc towards lower right and stops before right ribs, forming a hold-ball gesture with the right, left palm upward and right palm downward. Weight is shifted on to right leg, and left foot is drawn beside the right, with toes on ground. Eyes on right hand. (Fig. 5)

2) Torso turns left, and left foot takes a step forward obliquely to the left, toes pointing forward as right leg straightens naturally, and left leg bends at knee to form a left bow step. Meanwhile, left arm is bent horizontally like a bow and thrusts forward with back of arm and hand at shoulder level, palm facing inward. Right hand drops to lower right beside right hip, with elbow slightly bent and palm downward. Eyes on left forearm. (Fig. 6)

3) Body turns left a little, and left arm is bent horizontally before left chest at shoulder level, palm downward. Right

7   8

hand draws an arc before abdomen to left and stops before left ribs, palm upward, forming a hold-ball gesture with the left. Meanwhile, right foot is drawn beside the left, toes on ground, and weight is shifted on to left leg. Eyes on left hand. (Fig. 7)

4) Torso turns right, and right foot takes a step forward obliquely to the right. Left heel treads backward as right leg bends at knee, forming a right bow step. Meanwhile, torso turns right further, facing forward, and right arm thrusts forward with back of hand at shoulder level, palm in. Left hand goes down beside left hip, palm downward with fingers pointing forward. Eyes on right forearm. (Fig. 8)

Remember:

In thrusting out right arm, both shoulders are lowered and arms rounded. The separation of hands, relaxation of waist and bending of leg must be coordinated. In the bow step of this form, the transverse (not the actual) distance between feet is about 10 cm. In drawing either

9 10

foot to the other as in 1) and 3). Once the shifting of weight, is mastered forward foot may move past the inside of the other without touching ground with toes.

5) Torso turns right a little, and right hand extends forward, turning palm downward, while left palm turns up, passing before abdomen, and moves up and forward under right forearm. Then as torso turns left, both hands swing down and backward in an arc passing before abdomen, until left hand is at shoulder level, palm upward, and right arm is bent horizontally before chest, palm facing in. Meanwhile, weight is shifted on to left leg. Eyes on left hand. (Fig. 9, 10, 11)

Remember:

In swinging back arms, do not lean forward, and keep buttocks in. The swinging arms should move with the turning torso in an arc. Right sole is flat on ground.

11 **12** **13**

6) Torso turns right a little, and left arm is drawn back bent at elbow, with left palm close to inside of right wrist (about 5cm apart). Torso turns right further, facing forward, and both hands gradually push forward, right palm in and left palm out, with forearms half rounded. Meanwhile, weight is slowly shifted forward to form a right bow step. Eyes on right wrist. (Figs. 12, 13)

Remember:

In pushing out, torso should remain erect. The pushing movement should be coordinated with relaxation of waist and bending of leg.

           14   15

7) Left hand extends forward obliquely to the left over right wrist until it is side by side with the right, palm downward. Right palm turns down and both hands separate shoulder-width apart. Then torso sits back, shifting weight on to left leg, and right toes turn up. Meanwhile, both arms bend at elbow and are drawn back before chest, palms down and forward; Eyes Front. (Figs. 14, 15, 16)

8) Still in motion, both hands draw back further and, passing before abdomen, push upward and forward, palms facing forward with wrists at shoulder level. Meanwhile, weight is shifted forward, and right leg bends to form a right bow step. Eyes front. (Fig. 17)

Remember:

In pushing forward, torso should be erect, waist and hips relaxed. The pushing movement should be coordinated with relaxation of waist and bending of leg gradually, with shoulders lowered and elbows hung loose. Both hands move in a curve.

16   17

All the movements are centered around waist section. Both arms moving around it should be naturally rounded and flexible. The leg in bending forward or backward should be agile and steady. In swinging arms or pushing out, rear heel should not budge.

18   19

Form 4 Single Whip

1) Torso sits back, shifting weight onto left leg, with right toes turned in. Meanwhile torso turns left, and both hands, the left on top, turn left in an arc until left arm is extended horizontal on the left, palm facing left, and right hand goes, passing abdomen, before left rib, palm in and obliquely upward. Eyes on left hand. (Figs. 18, 19)

2) Weight is gradually shifted on to right leg, and torso turns right with left foot drawn beside the right, toes on ground. Meanwhile, right hand draws an upper right arc, palm turning outward, until it turns into a "hook-hand" with arm extended at shoulder level. Left hand also draws an upper right curve in front of abdomen and stops before right shoulder, palm in. Eyes on left hand. (Figs. 20, 21)

3) Torso turns left a little, and left foot takes a step forward obliquely to the left, toes pointing slightly left as right heel treads backward to form a left bow step. While weight is shifting on to left leg, left palm turns with torso and pushes

20   21   22

out, facing forward, with fingers at eye level and arm slightly bent. Eyes on left hand. (Fig. 22)

Remember:

At completion, keep torso erect and waist relaxed. Right elbow is bent down a bit, and left elbow is in vertical line with left knee, with both shoulders lowered. In pushing out, left palm should turn out gradually with the movement of torso, and not too fast or abruptly. In all the transitional movements, the upper and lower halves of body must be well coordinated. If you start facing south, the direction of "Single Whip" is about 15' northeast.

23   24

Form 5   Raise Hands

Right leg bends slowly, and torso sits back and turns right, with left toes turned in, then shifting weight on to left leg. Meanwhile, right "hook-hand" turns into an open palm and, moving from the right stops in front of face with fingers pointing up at eyebrow level. Left hand is drawn inside right elbow before chest, palm to palm, with the right. At the same time, right foot is lifted to shift in front of the left, heel on ground, in a right hollow step. Eyes on right forefinger. (Figs. 23, 24)

Remember:
> In shifting weight, torso must be kept naturally steady, with buttocks in. As right heel touches ground, right knee bends slightly with shoulders lowered in relaxation, arms slightly bent and elbows hung down. Chest muscles are relaxed. If you start facing south, the direction of the present form is about 30' southwest.

25 26 27

Form 6   White Crane Spreading Wings

Torso turns left, and hands move together to form a hold-ball gesture in front, left hand on top. Meanwhile, right foot shifts a little backward with toes turned in. Then torso turns right and then left a little, facing forward. Meanwhile, hands separate, the right coming up before right temple, palm facing left and slightly in, as the left drops before left hip, palm downward with fingers pointing forward. At the same time, weight is shifted back on to right leg, and left foot is shifted in front of body, toes on ground, to form a left hollow step. Eyes front. (Figs. 25 – 27)

Remember:

> On completion, you have turned back, facing due east. Do not thrust out chest; keep both arms rounded, and left knee slightly bent. The shifting back of weight and movements of hands should be coordinated.

28   29

Form 7   Brush Knee and Twist Step — Left

1) Right hand drops and swings back and up in an arc, elbow slightly bent, until it is outside right shoulder at ear level, palm obliquely upward. Left hand comes up from left and down to right in an arc, stopping before right chest, palm obliquely downward. Meanwhile, torso turns first a little left and then right, and left foot is drawn beside the right, toes on ground. Eyes on right hand. (Figs. 28 — 30)

30   31

2) Torso turns left, and left foot takes a step forward obliquely to the left, as right is straightened naturally to form a left bow step. Meanwhile, right hand is drawn back and pushes out beside ear at nose level, and left hand, brushing over left knee, drops beside left hip with fingers pointing forward. Eyes on right fingers. (Fig. 31)

Remember:

In pushing out right hand, lower shoulder and loosen elbow, with palm raised with ease. Do not lean forward or backward, and movement of torso should be co-ordinated with relaxation of waist and bending of leg. In the bow step of this form, transverse distance between heels is about 30 cm. Once the shifting of weight is mastered, the forward stepping foot may move without touching ground with toes, but it must pass the inside of the other (pausing in slow motion when necessary) before going forward, and body must be balanced. (Hereafter, the same is omitted to avoid redundancy.)

32   33

Form 8   Hands Strumming the Lute

Right foot takes half a step after the left, and torso immediately sits back, half facing right and shifting weight on to right leg. Left foot is lifted to shift forward, heel on ground, with toes turned up in a hollow step. Meanwhile, left hand comes up from left to front in an arc at nose level, palm facing right and elbow slightly bent, and right hand is drawn back beside left elbow, palm facing left. Eyes on left forefinger. (Figs. 32, 33)

Remember:

> Keep body naturally steady, with buttocks in. Lower shoulders and loosen elbows with chest relaxed. In coming up, left hand should not come up straight, but in a curve upward from left, and then forward. In stepping forward, right foot should land on heel first, before setting firm on ground. Shift-back of weight should be coordinated with Torso's half turn and the movements of arms.

34   35

Form 9 Brush Knee and Twist Step — Left and Right

1) Right hand drops and swings back and up in an arc, elbow slightly bent, until it is outside right shoulder at ear level, palm obliquely upward. Left hand comes up from left and down to right in an arc, stopping before right chest, palm obliquely downward. Meanwhile, torso turns right, and left foot is drawn beside the right, toes on ground. Eyes on right hand. (Fig. 34)

2) Torso turns left, and left foot takes a step forward obliquely to the left to form a left bow step. Meanwhile, right hand is drawn back and pushes out beside ear at nose level, and left hand, brushing over left knee, drops beside left hip. Eyes on right fingers. (Fig. 35)

36　　　　　　　37　　　　　　　38

3) Right leg slowly bends at knee, and torso sits back, shifting weight on to right leg, and turns left, with left toes turned up and out a little. Then left sole sets firm on ground, and left knee bends forward, shifting weight on to left leg; right foot is drawn beside the left, toes on ground. Meanwhile, left palm turns out and comes back and up in an arc, elbow slightly bent, until it is outside left shoulder at ear level, palm obliquely upward. Right hand comes up and turns down to left in an arc, with the turn of body, and stops before left shoulder, palm obliquely downward. Eyes on left hand. (Figs. 36 – 38)

39   40

4) The same as 2), only with left and right reversed. (Fig. 39)

5) The same as 3), only with left and right reversed. (Fig. 40-42)

6) The same as 2). (Fig. 43)
   Remember:
   "Brush Knee and Twist Step — Right" is the same as Form 7 only with left and right reversed.

41

42

43

44 45

Form 10 Hands Strumming the Lute

Movements and points to remember are the same as Form 8. (Figs. 44, 45)

46   47

Form 11 Step up, Parry and Punch

1) Body turns left, and left toes turn out and set firm with sole on ground. Meanwhile, left palm turns down, with left arm bent horizontally before chest, and right palm clenches into a fist, which drops to the left in an arc before left ribs with knuckles on top. At the same time, weight is shifted forward onto left leg, with the right slightly bent, heel raised and turned out. Eyes on left hand. (Fig. 46)

2) Torso turns right, and right fist comes up before chest and thrusts out, like in a backhand, kunckles down. Left hand naturally drops beside left hip, while right foot takes a step forward with toes turned out. Eyes on right fist. (Fig. 47)

        48   49

3) Weight is shifted on to right leg, and left hand comes up and turns left and then forward in an arc to parry an imaginary blow, palm facing forward and down. Meanwhile left foot takes a step forward, heel on ground, and right fist is drawn from right in an arc beside right side of waist, knuckles down. Eyes on left hand. (Fig. 48)

4) Left leg bends forward to form a left bow step, while right fist strikes forward at chest level with knuckles facing right, and left hand is pulled back beside right forearm. Eyes on right fist. (Fig. 49)

Remember:

Hold torso erect and clench fist loosely. While drawing back fist, right forearm should turn first slowly anti-clockwise and then clockwise, ending beside right side of waist, knuckles down. While the fist strikes out, right shoulder should follow the movement and extend a bit forward. Keep shoulder and elbow low with forearm slightly bent. Transverse distance between heels in bow step is the same as in Form 3, about 10 cm.

50   51

Form 12 Apparent Close-Up

1) Left hand extends forward from below right wrist, which opens into a palm. Gradually both palms turn up, separate and are drawn back slowly. Meanwhile torso sits back with left toes raised, shifting weight on to right leg. Eyes front. (Figs. 50, 51)

52   53

2) Both palms, turning down before chest shoulder-width apart, push down past abdomen and then up and forward, facing out. Meanwhile, left leg bends forward to form a left bow step. Eyes front. (Figs. 52, 53)

Remember:

While sitting back, waist and hips must be relaxed, and torso should not lean backward. Keep buttocks in. Do not pull straight back, when withdrawing arms, and let shoulders and elbows extend freely outward a little. The extended hands should be no farther than shoulder-width apart.

54 55

Form 13 Cross Hands

1) Right leg bends at knee a little, and weight is shifted on to it, left toes turn in as torso turns right, with right arm swinging horizontally to right in an arc, so that both arms are spread out at shoulder level, palms facing forward and elbows slightly bent. Meanwhile, right toes are turned a bit out to form a side bow step. Eyes on right hand. (Figs. 54, 55)

56   57

2) Weight is slowly shifted on to left leg and right toes turn in. Right foot is then drawn towards the left so that they are shoulder-width apart, and both legs gradually straighten into a parallel stance with toes pointing forward. Meanwhile both hands are lowered and crossed before chest, the right in front of the left, with arms rounded and wrists at shoulder level, both palms facing in. Eyes front. (Figs. 56, 57)

Remember:

Do not lean forward when separating or crossing hands. Turn in right toes before drawing back right foot. While in a parallel stance, keep body naturally erect, with head straight and chin slightly in. Keep arms rounded in a comfortable position, with shoulders and elbows down.

58   59

Form 14 Return to Mountain with Tiger

1) Weight is shifted slightly to the right, and left toes turn in. Then both legs bend at knee, shifting weight on to left leg. Torso turns left, and left hand goes down before chest and then up to the left in an arc, until it is at shoulder level, palm obliquely upward. Right arm is bent at elbow, and right hand drawn back before left shoulder, palm obliquely downward. Eyes on left hand. (Fig. 58)

2) Torso turns slightly right, and right foot takes a step backward and right, bending knee to form a right bow step. Meanwhile, right hand, following the turning body, goes down, brushing over right leg, and stops beside right knee. Left arm is bent at elbow, and left hand pushes out beside ear at nose level. Eyes on left hand. (Fig. 59)

Remember:

Shift weight onto right leg, before turning in left foot and crouch. The brushing right hand is higher than in Form 9 (Right), and stops beside right knee. Turning of body and pushing out must be coordinated. If you start facing south, the direction of this form is about 30' north-west.

60   61

Form 15 Obliquely Grasp Peacock's Tail

Torso turns slightly right, and right hand comes up to shoulder level, palm obliquely downward. Meanwhile, left palm turns up and moves under right arm. The rest goes on like in Form 3, only the direction is the same as Form 14. (Figs. 60 – 65)

Remember:

> Except the pushing out with back of hand, the rest are the same as in Form 3 (Right), only the direction is obique (diagonal).

62

63

64

65

66   67

Form 16 Fist under Elbow

1) Torso sits back, shifting weight slowly onto left leg, and right toes turn in. Meanwhile, torso turns left, and both hands move in curves to the left, the left horizontally until arm is extended beside left shoulder, and the right down in front of abdomen, ending before left ribs, palm facing in and obliquely upward. Eyes on left hand. (Fig. 66)

2) Weight is gradually shifted on to right leg, and torso turns right, while left foot is drawn beside the right, toes on ground. Meanwhile, right hand comes up in an arc, until it is extended at shoulder level on right side, palm facing out, and left hand, at the same time, drops before abdomen and comes up in an arc before right shoulder, palm facing in. Eyes on right hand. (Fig. 67)

68 **69**

3) Left foot takes a step forward obliquely to the left, toes turned out, and weight is shifted as body turns left. Right foot, following body movement, takes half a step forward obliquely to the left behind left foot. Meanwhile, left hand also moves left and is drawn back beside left side of waist, palm up, and right arm, drawing a big arc to the left, is bent horizontally before chest. Eyes front. (Figs. 68, 69)

Remember:

Stepping out by left foot and movements of arms should be coordinated with left-turn of body. Right foot moves forward after left foot is well set on ground.

70

4) From beside waist, left hand extends forward over right wrist with fingers pointing up, palm facing right, at nose level. Right palm closes into a fist, which is drawn under left elbow, knuckles facing right. Meanwhile, weight is shifted on to right leg, and left foot takes half a step forward, with heel on ground and knee slightly bent, forming a left hollow step. Eyes on left palm. (Fig. 70)

Remember:
Hold body naturally erect. While left palm extends forward, weight is on right leg, with left leg slightly bent.

71   72

Form 17 Slip Back Arm — Left and Right

1) Right fist opens into a palm, which is turned upward, moves down before abdomen and comes up behind in an arc until arm is extended horizontally, slightly bent; then left palm turns up. Left knee is relaxed, and, following the right-turn of torso, eyes are first right, and then front on left hand. (Figs. 71, 72)

2) Right arm, bent at elbow, moves forward as hand passes right ear and pushes out, palm facing forward. Left arm, bent at elbow, withdraws, palm upward, to the side of left ribs. Meanwhile, left leg is slightly raised to take a step back obliquely to the left, with sole on ground and gradually set firm, and weight is shifted on to left leg, forming a right hollow step with right foot naturally turned straight. Eyes on right hand. (Figs. 73, 74)

3) Torso turns slightly left, while left hand comes up behind in an arc, extended horizontally, palm upward. Then right palm turns up. Following the turn of torso, eyes are first left, and then front on right hand. (Fig. 75)

73

74

75

76　　　　　　　　　77

4) The same as 2), only with left and right reversed. (Figs. 76, 77)
5) The same as 3), only with left and right reversed. (Fig. 78)
6) The same as 2). (Figs. 79, 80)

Remember:
  The hand pushing forward should not be stretched straight; the withdrawing hand should not be drawn straight back, but in a curve. In pushing forward, turn at waist with hips relaxed and both hands moving at an even pace, avoiding stiffness. In retreat, land on ball of foot first, gradually setting the sole firm on ground, while the foot in front turns naturally straight in line. The retreating left foot should turn obliquely left, the retreating right obliquely right. Also, avoid ups and downs in backward movement, and keep steady. The front knee of hollow step should not be kept stiffly straight. In following movement of body, eyes should first turn left and then right about 90' before setting on the front hand.

78 79

80

81   82

Form 18 Oblique Flying

1) Torso turns slightly left, and left hand swings back and upward in an arc until it is horizontally extended, palm obliquely upward, as right wrist relaxes with palm obliquely downward. Eyes turn left first with body, and then front on right hand. (Fig. 81)
2) With left hand drawing an arc, left arm is drawn horizontally before chest, palm downward, and right hand drops down in an arc before abdomen ending palm to palm with the left. Right foot is drawn beside left heel, toes on ground. (Fig. 82)

83   84

3) Body pivots to the right on ball of left foot, twisting right foot outward, and right foot takes a step forward to the right, to form a right bow step, facing forward and right. Meanwhile, hands separate in opposite directions, the right coming up to eye level, palm obliquely upward, and the left going down beside left hip, palm down with fingers pointing forward. Eyes on right hand. (Figs. 83, 84)

Remember:

Do not turn so fast, but steadily and gracefully. If you start facing south, the direction of this form is about 30' southwest.

85   86

Form 19 Raise Hands

Left foot takes half a step forward, shifting weight on to left leg, then right foot is raised to land on heel with knee slightly bent, forming a right hollow step. Meanwhile, right palm swings right a little and lowers to eyebrow level in front, with palm facing left, and left hand comes up inside right elbow before chest, palm to palm with the right. Eyes on right hand. (Figs. 85, 86)

Remember:

The same as in Form 5.

87 88 89

Form 20 White Crane Spreading Wings

    Movements and points to remember are the same as Form 6. (Figs. 87 – 89)

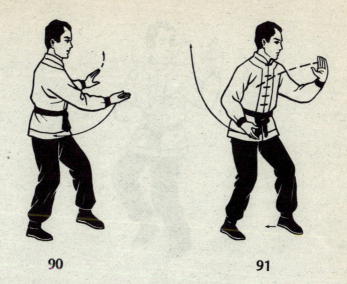

90 91

Form 21 Brush Knee and Twist Step — Left

Movements and points to remember are the same as Form 7. (Figs. 90 – 93)

92

93

94   95

Form 22   Needle at Sea Bottom

Right foot takes half a step forward, shifting weight on to right leg, and left foot moves forward a little, toes on ground, to form a left hollow step. Meanwhile, body turns slightly right, and right hand goes down in front of body, and draws up beside right ear. Then as body turns slightly left, it thrusts slanting down in front of body, palm facing left with fingers pointing obliquely down. At the same time, left hand makes an arc in front, down beside left hip, palm downward with fingers pointing forward. Eyes front and downward. (Figs. 94, 95)

Remember:

Turn body first right, and then left. Do not lean too far out or bend head forward. Keep buttocks in and left knee slightly bent.

96

Form 23 Flash Out Arms

Torso turns slightly right, and left foot takes a step forward to form a left bow step. Meanwhile, right hand is drawn up, bending elbow, until it stops above right temple, palm turned obliquely upward with thumb down. Left hand comes up before chest and pushes forward at nose level, palm outward. Eyes on left hand. (Fig. 96)

Remember:

At completion, hold torso erect in a natural position with waist and hips relaxed. Do not straighten left arm. Keep spinal muscles extended. Movements of hands and legs should be coordinated, and the transverse distance between heels should not exceed 10 cm in the bow step.

97   98

Form 24   Turn, Sidle and Punch

1) Right leg bends slowly, and weight is shifting on to it, as left toes turn in. Body turns right, and weight is shifted on to left leg. Meanwhile, right hand swings to the right and down, clenching into a fist, in front of abdomen and curves in before left ribs, knuckles up. Left hand is lifted above forehead with arm rounded, palm obliquely upward. Eyes front. (Fig. 97)

2) Body turns right further, and right foot is lifted to take a step forward obliquely to the right, toes turned slightly right, forming a right bow step. Meanwhile, right hand turns knuckles down and thrusts out backhand, and left hand falls from above down beside right elbow. Eyes on right fist. (Fig. 98)

Remember:

    First draw back right foot, without touching ground, before stepping out. The bow step and backhand thrust should be coordinated. The direction of bow step is about 15' northwest.

99　　　　　　　　100

Form 25 Step Up, Parry and Punch

1) Left leg bends, and weight is shifted on to left leg. Body turns slightly left, and right foot is drawn back beside the left, toes on ground. Meanwhile, right fist turns knuckles down, goes down, passing abdomen, to the left in an arc beside left ribs, and left arm is drawn back in an arc and bent horizontally before chest, palm downward. Eyes front. (Fig. 99)

2) Body pivots to the right, and right leg moves out, turning toes outward. Meanwhile, right fist passes in front of chest and thrusts out backhand, knuckles down. Left hand drops from outside right arm down beside left hip, palm downward with fingers pointing forward. Eyes on right fist. (Fig. 100)

          101   102

3) Weight is shifted on to right leg, and body turns right, as left foot takes a step forward. Left hand comes up in an arc, parrying forward, palm forward and obliquely down. Meanwhile, right fist is drawn from the right in an arc beside right side of waist, knuckles down. Eyes on left hand. (Fig. 101)

4) Left leg bends forward into a left bow step, and right fist thrusts out, knuckles facing right, chest high, as left hand is drawn inside right forearm. Eyes front. (Fig. 102)

Remember:
    The same as in Form 11. When skilled, right foot may be drawn beside the left without touching ground.

103　　　　　　　　　　104

Form 26 Step Up and Grasp Peacock's Tail

1) Weight is shifted slightly back, and body turns half facing left with toes turned outward. Meanwhile, left hand swings down left and comes up behind in an arc, drawn horizontally in front of chest, palm downward, and right fist opens into a palm, which goes down in an arc ending before abdomen, facing up and forming a hold-ball gesture with the left. Right foot moves forward beside the left, toes on ground. Eyes on left hand. (Fig. 103)

2) The rest are the same as Form 3, Fig. 8 – 17. (Figs. 104 – 113)

   Remember:
   The same as in Form 3. When skilled, right foot may pass beside the left without touching ground with toes.

105

106

107

108

109

110

111 112 113

114   115

Form 27 Single Whip

Movements and points to remember are the same as Form 4. (Figs. 114 – 118)

116

117

118

119 120

Form 28 Wave Hands like Clouds

1) Weight is shifted on to right leg, and body gradually turns right with left toes turned in. Left hand makes an arc upward past abdomen and ends in front of right shoulder, palm turned obliquely in. Meanwhile, right hand opens, turning palm out. Eyes on left hand. (Figs. 119, 120)

          121   122

2) Torso gradually turns left, shifting weight on to left leg. Left hand moves left in an arc past face with palm turning slowly out, and right hand makes an arc past abdomen to left shoulder, palm turned obliquely in. Meanwhile, right foot is drawn beside the left so that they are parallel and 10 – 20 cm. apart. Eyes on right hand. (Figs. 121, 122)

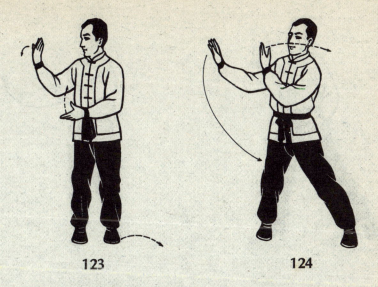

123   124

3) Torso turns gradually right, shifting weight on to right leg. Right hand moves on to the right past face, palm turned out while left hand makes an arc upward past abdomen and up to right shoulder, palm turned in obliquely. Left foot then takes a side step. Eyes on left hand. (Figs. 123, 124)

        125   126

4) The same as 2). (Figs. 125, 126)

5) The same as 3). (Figs. 127, 128)

6) The same as 2). (Figs. 129, 130)

Remember:

    Lumbar spine is the axis for body turns. Keep waist and hips relaxed and avoid sudden ups and downs in stance. Movements of arms should be natural and circular at an even pace, following the waist. Keep body steady when moving lower limbs, with ball of foot on ground first before setting the sole firm. Eyes should follow the hand which moves past face. In order to complete the whole series where you start, repeat the movements 5 times. In taking the final side step, right toes should be slightly turned in to get ready for the coming Single Whip.

127

128

129

130

131   132

Form 29 Single Whip

On completion of the fifth "Move Hands", right hand moves up right, turning into a "hook-hand", while left foot moves out to form a "Single Whip". The rest are the same as Form 4. (Figs. 131 – 133)

133

134   135

Form 30 High Pat on Horse

1) Right foot takes half a step forward, and body turns slightly right, shifting weight gradually on to right leg. Right "hook-hand" opens into a palm, and both palms turn up with elbows slightly bent and left heel raised gradually off ground. Eyes front-left. (Fig. 134)

2) Torso turns slightly left, facing forward, and right hand moves past right ear and pushes forward, palm out with fingers up at eye level. Left hand is drawn in front of left hip, palm upward. Meanwhile, left foot moves slightly forward, toes on ground, into a left hollow step. Eyes on right hand. (Fig. 135)

Remember:

Hold torso erect and relaxed, and shoulders low with right elbow slightly bent down. Do not let body rise or fall when shifting weight on to right leg.

136   137

Form 31 Right Kick

1) Cross hands by lifting left hand, palm upward, and extending it over the back of right wrist. Then hands separate, each drawing an arc downward on either side with palm turned gradually down, and cross again in front with both palms in. Meanwhile left foot takes a step forward to the left, toes turned out, to form a left bow step, and then right foot is drawn beside the left, toes on ground. Eyes right. (Figs. 136 – 138)

138   **139**

2) Both arms separate in opposite directions in an arc, extending horizontally sideways with elbows slightly bent, palms outward. Meanwhile, right leg is raised bent at knee, and kicks out slowly with shank, while toes are held down. Eyes on right hand. (Fig. 139)

Remember:

Keep your balance, and do not lean either forward or backward. Wrists are level with shoulders, which are lowered with elbows, when hands separate. Left foot is slightly bent as right foot kicks out; right arm should correspond to right leg in position, the direction being about 30' southeast. Separation of hands and feet must be well coordinated.

140   141

Form 32 Left Kick

1) Right Leg is drawn back and then takes a step forward to the right to form a right bow step, half facing right. Left hand moves from left before chest, and extends forward, palm turned up, crossing over the right. Both hand separate in opposite directions, and, each going down in a curve on either side, they cross again in front, the left before the right and both palms in. Meanwhile, left foot is drawn beside the right, toes on ground. Eyes front-left. (Figs. 140, 141)

142

2) Both arms separate in opposite directions in an arc, extending horizontally sideways with elbows slightly bent, palms outward. Meanwhile, left leg is raised bent at knee, and kicks out with shank; while toes are held down. Eyes on left hand. (Fig. 142)

Remember:
  The same as in previous form, only with left and right reversed. The direction is about 30' northeast.

143   144   145

Form 33 Turn and Kick with Left Heel

1) Left foot lands behind the right, toes on ground, while both hands swing down and close before abdomen, the left before the right and palms in. Eyes on left hand. (Fig. 143)

2) Body pivots about on ball of right foot anticlockwise, Both hands are raised crossed before chest and then separate in opposite directions in an arc, extending sideways at shoulder level with elbows slightly bent, palms out. Meanwhile, left leg is raised bent at knee and kicks out to the left with heel. Eyes on left hand. (Figs. 144, 145)

Remember:

Keep body balanced and erect. Both wrists are at shoulder level when hands separate. While kicking out, the standing leg is slightly bent, and left toes are drawn backward with force concentrated on heel. Left arm and left leg correspond in position. If you start facing south, the direction of the kick is due west. Separating hands must be coordinated with the kick.

146 147

Form 34 Brush Knee and Twist Step — Left and Right

1) Left foot lands and takes a step forward obliquely to the left, forming a left bow step. Meanwhile, left arm bends at elbow, and left hand is drawn in an arc to right shoulder as right palm turns up. Then left hand brushes over left knee and stops beside left hip, and right hand pushes out from beside right ear. Eyes on right hand. (Figs. 146, 147)

2) The rest are the same as Form 9, 3) and 4). (Figs. 148 — 151)

148

149

150

151

152　　　　　　　153　　　　　　　154

Form 35 Step Up and Punch Down

Weight is shifted backward a little, and right toes turn out as body turns right. Meanwhile, left hand moves back before right shoulder as right hand is raised from behind, clenching into a fist. Then left foot takes a step forward to form a left bow step, and left hand, brushing over left knee, drops beside left hip as right fist punches down obliquely forward, knuckles up. Eyes front and downward. (Figs. 152 — 154)

Remember:

Keep body erect, and waist and hips relaxed. Right shoulder should not go down with the punch.

155   156   157

Form 36 White Snake Showing Tongue

1) Weight is shifted back, and right fist is drawn up with forearm acrossing chest, knuckles down. Left hand is raised in an arc, stopping above forehead. Meanwhile, left toes turn in and body turns right, shifting weight on to left leg, and right foot is drawn back to take a small step backward to the right with knee bent and toes turned slightly right, while weight is still mainly on left leg. At the same time, right fist thrusts out backhand in the same direction as right foot, knuckles down and elbow bent down, and left hand drops inside right forearm, palm downward. Eyes on right fist. (Figs. 155 – 158)

158　　　　　　159　　　　　　160

2) Left hand extends over right fist, palm forward, and right fist opens into a palm, which is drawn beside right side of waist, palm upward. Meanwhile, right leg bends forward to form a right bow step. Eyes on left hand. (Fig.159)

3) Weight is shifted back on to left leg, and right foot shifts back a little, heel slightly raised, forming a right hollow step. Meanwhile, right hand closes into a fist and thrusts out under the left chest high, knuckles facing right, and left hand is drawn inside right forearm. Eyes on right fist. (Fig. 160)

Remember:

Hold body erect. Left hand pushes out slightly to the right in a curve. While thrusting out, do not straighten right arm and keep shoulder and elbow low. In retreat, turn up toes before withdrawing right foot, and keep your balance. If you start facing south, the direction is about 15' south east.

161   162

Form 37 Step Up, Parry and Punch

Body turns left, and right fist goes down left passing abdomen and then up before stopping beside the left of waist, knuckles up. Right foot is drawn beside the left, toes on ground, and left palm, turning up, goes backward and up before turning forward, ending with left forearm bent horizontally before chest, palm downward. The rest are the same as Form 11, 2) — 4). (Figs. 161 — 164)

Remember:

The same as in Form 11. When skilled, right foot may be drawn back without touching ground with toes.

163 164

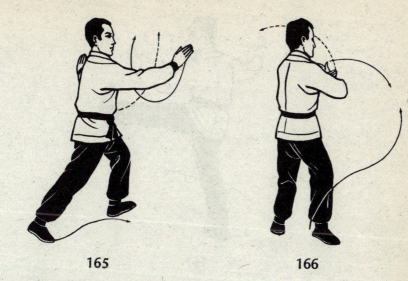

165   166

Form 38 Kick with Right Heel

1) Both hands are raised and spread out, and after going down in an arc, they cross before chest, the right in front of the left and palms in. Meanwhile, weight is shifted back a little, and left toes turn slightly out. Then weight is shifted on to left leg, and right foot takes a step forward beside the left, toes on ground. Eyes right and obliquely forward. (Figs. 165, 166)

2) Right leg is raised bent at knee, and right foot slowly kicks out obliquely to the right, toes turned backward. Meanwhile, hands separate in opposite directions until arms are spread out with elbows slightly bent. Eyes on right hand. (Fig. 167)

Remember:

The same as in Form 31, only the force of kick is concentrated on heel.

167

168

Form 39 Sidle Left To Tame Tiger

1) Right foot lands behind left heel in a cross-step, while left hand moves from left to right in an arc in front, stopping beside right forearm. Eyes on right hand. (Fig. 168)

169

2) Left leg is raised bent at knee, and left foot takes a side step. Meanwhile, Torso turns back anticlockwise, and left knee bends to form a left bow step. At the same time, both hands go down before abdomen and up to the left, the right turning into a fist before left side of chest, knuckles up, while the left turning into a fist above left temple, Knuckles backward, in a vertical line with the right. Eyes turn with body before settling forward obliquely to the right. (Fig. 169)

Remember:

The distance between crossed feet should be controlled. At completion, the direction of left bow step should be vertical to the transverse axis. If you start facing south, the direction of the left bow step is due north with body facing northeast. Both arms should be rounded, with muscles relaxed, and so are the waist and hips in bow step.

170 171 172

Form 40 Sidle Right To Tame Tiger

Weight is shifted back, and left toes turn in as torso turns right, shifting weight again on to left leg. Then right knee is raised, and right foot takes a side step, bending the leg into a right bow step. Meanwhile, both fists open into palms and go down before abdomen and up to the right in an arc, the left turning into a fist again before right side of chest, knuckles up, while the right turning into a fist above right temple, knuckles backward, in a vertical line. Eyes to the left forward obliquely. (Figs. 170 – 172)

Remember:

The same as in previous form, only there is no cross-step and left and right are reversed. The direction of bow step at completion is due south, body facing south-east.

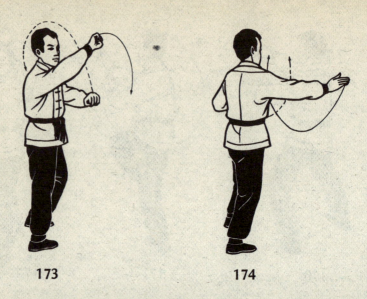

173   174

Form 41 About-Turn and Kick with Right Heel

1) Left knee bends, and right toes turn in. Body turns left, and left toes turn out, shifting weight on to left leg. Left fist is raised with the turn of body, and both arms separate, spreading out with fists opened into palms. They come together and cross before chest again, the right before the left with palms in. Meanwhile, right foot is drawn beside the left, toes on ground. Eyes to the right forward obliquely. (Figs. 173 – 175)

Remember:

When body turns left, and weight is on both legs, turn left toes out naturally.

175 176

2) The kick with right heel is the same as Form 38. (Fig. 176)
   Remember:
   The same as in Form 31, only concentrating the force on heel.

177   178   179

Form 42 Strike Opponent's Ears with Both Fists

1) Right leg is raised bent at knee, and left hand comes up from behind and turns forward in front of body. Both palms turned up, and then go down in an arc on both sides of right knee. Eyes front. (Fig. 177)

2) Right foot lands in front obliquely to the right, shifting weight forward to form a right bow step, facing forward obliquely to the right. Meanwhile, both hands drop, gradually clenching into fists, which swerve up and forward from the sides to the front in a pincer movement at ear level, knuckles obliquely upward. The distance between fists is about 10 – 20 cm. Eyes on right fist. (Figs. 178, 179)

Remember:

At completion, hold head and neck erect, and keep waist and hips relaxed, fists loosely clenched. Shoulders are lowered and elbows hung slightly bent. If you start facing south, the direction is the same as the previous form, i.e., southeast.

180　　　　　　　　　181

Form 43　Kick with Left Heel

1) Weight is shifted back, and right toes turn out. Both fists open into palms and spread out before they turn down in an arc and cross before chest, the left before the right, with palms in. Meanwhile, weight is again shifted on to right leg, and left foot is drawn beside the right, toes on ground. Eyes to the left forward obliquely. (Figs. 180, 181)

182

2) Arms spread out again slowly with elbows slightly bent, palms outward. Meanwhile, left leg is slowly raised and kicks out obliquely to the left, toes turned backward. Eyes on left hand. (Fig. 182)

Remember:

The same as in Form 32, except the direction, which is due east if you start facing south.

183   184   185

Form 44 Turn and Kick with Right Heel

1) Left leg is raised bent at knee and lands with left foot outside the right. While left leg is going down, body pivots to the right on right toes about 270'. As left foot lands, weight is shifted on to left leg, with right heel slightly raised. Meanwhile, both hands are lowered in an arc and cross in front of chest, the right before the left. Eyes to the right forward obliquely. (Figs. 183, 184)

2) Both arms spread out with elbows slightly bent, palms outward. Meanwhile, right leg is raised bent at knee, and right foot slowly kicks out obliquely to the right, toes turned backward. Eyes on right hand. (Fig. 185)

Remember:

The same as previous form, only with left and right reversed. The direction of the kick is due east.

186   187

Form 45 Step Up, Parry and Punch

1) Right leg is raised bent at knee, and landing with toes on ground, takes a step forward with toes turned out. (When skilled, right foot may step out without touching ground.) Meanwhile, right palm drops clenching into a fist, and passing before abdomen, thrusts out backhand, knuckles down, and left palm is drawn back with elbow bent, to left side, palm downward. Eyes on right fist. (Figs. 186, 187)

188 189

2) The rest are the same as Form 11, 3 and 4) (Figs. 188, 189)
Remember:
The same as in Form 11.

Form 46 Apparent Close-Up

The same as Form 12. (Figs. 190 – 193)

Form 47 Cross Hands

The same as Form 13. (Figs. 194 — 197)

194   195

196   197

Form 48 Return to Mountain with Tiger

The same as Form 14. (Figs. 198, 199)

198

199

Form 49 Obliquely Grasp Peacock's Tail

The same as Form 15. (Fig. 200 – 205)

200

201

202

203

204

205

206   207

Form 50 Side-Step Single Whip

The same as Form 4, except that left foot takes a step due south to from a left bow step, the direction being perpendicular to body axis, facing due south. (Figs. 206 – 209)

208

209

210   211

Form 51 Parting Wild Horse's Mane — Left and Right

1) Weight is shifted slightly on to left leg, and body turns slightly left. Left arm is drawn horizontally in front of chest, and right hook-hand opens into a palm, which passes in front of body and goes under the right in an arc, forming a hold-ball gesture, left palm down, chest high and right palm up, waist high. Meanwhile, right foot is drawn beside the left, toes on ground. (Fig. 210)

2) Torso turns slightly right, and right foot steps forward obliquely to the right as left heel treads backward (without moving), straightening left leg into a right bow step. Meanwhile, as torso goes on turning right, both hands gradually separate until the right is in front of eyes, palm obliquely upward and elbow slightly bent, and the left falls beside left hip, elbow also bent slightly, with palm downward and fingers pointing forward. Eyes on right hand. (Fig. 211)

212 **213** **214**

3) Torso gradually sits back, shifting weight on to left leg, and right toes turn up, slightly outward. (about 45' − 60').
Right sole is set firm on ground, as right leg slowly bends forward and body turns right, shifting weight on to right leg again. Meanwhile, right arm is drawn horizontally before chest, palm down, and left hand comes up in an arc under the right, forming a hold-ball gesture. Then left foot is drawn beside the right, toes on ground. Eyes on right hand. (Figs. 212 − 214)

215　　　　　　　216　　　　　　　217

4) Left leg moves forward obliquely to the left, extending right leg to form a left bow step. Meanwhile, as torso turns left, both hands gradually separate until the left is in front of eyes, palm obliquely upward and elbow slightly bent, and the right falls beside right hip, elbow also bent slightly, with palm downward and fingers pointing forward. Eyes on left hand. (Fig. 215)

5) The same as 3), only with left and right reversed. (Figs. 216 − 218)

        218   219

6) The same as 4), only with left and right reversed. (Fig. 219)

Remember:

Do not lean forward or backward, and chest must be fully relaxed. Arms should remain rounded when separated. Body turns with lumbar section as the axis. In bow step, the transverse distance between heels is about 30 cm. The bow step and parting of hands should go together at an even pace. In stepping out, the foot may not touch ground at all, but must pass the inside of the supporting foot to maintain balance.

220 221 222

Form 52 Step Up and Grasp Peacock's Tail
1) Torso sits back, shifting weight on to left leg with right toes turned up and slightly outward. Then right leg bends forward, and body turns right, shifting weight on to right leg. Meanwhile, right palm turns down and is drawn before chest with arm horizontally bent, and left hand passes abdomen and goes up and right in an arc under the right, forming a hold-ball gesture palm to palm. Left foot takes a step forward beside the right, toes on ground. Eyes on right hand. (Figs. 220 – 222)

      223   224   225

2) Left foot steps forward obliquely to the left, forming a left bow step, while left arm thrusts out backhand obliquely to the left at shoulder level, and right hand drops down right beside right hip, palm down. Eyes on left forearm. (Fig. 223)

3) Torso sits back, and left toes turn out as body turns left. Meanwhile, left palm turns down and is drawn before chest with arm horizontally bent, and right hand passes abdomen in an arc to form a hold-ball gesture with the left. Right foot takes a step forward beside the left, toes on ground. Eyes on left hand. (Figs. 224, 225) The rest are the same as Form 26. (Figs. 226 — 234) When skilled, the forward going foot may move ahead without touching ground.

226

227

228

229

230 231 232

233 234

Form 53 Single Whip

The same as Form 4. (Figs. 235 — 239)

235   236   237

238   239

240   241   242

Form 54 Working as Shuttles (at 4 Angles)

1) Weight is shifted slightly backward, with left toes turn in, and is shifted again on to left leg, and right heel is twisted in on toes. Then body turns right and backward, twisting two bent legs in a crossed position. Meanwhile, right hand opens into a palm, with arm drawn before chest horizontally bent, facing down, and left hand goes down from left in an arc before abdomen, palm up, forming a hold-ball gesture palm to palm. Then left foot takes a step forward obliquely to the left, forming a left bow step, and left hand is raised before left temple, palm obliquely upward, as right hand pushes forward at nose level. Eyes on right hand. (Figs. 240 – 242)

243 244 245

2) Weight is shifted on to right leg, and left toes turn in. Body turns right and backward, shifting weight onto left leg again, and right foot is drawn beside the left, heel slightly raised. Meanwhile, left hand drops with arm horizontally bent before chest, and right hand is lowered before abdomen, palm up, forming a hold-ball gesture with the left. Then body pivots about clockwise on left toes, and right foot steps forward obliquely to right, bending leg into a right bow step. Right hand is raised before right temple, palm obliquely upward, and left hand pushes out. Eyes on left hand. (Figs. 243 — 245)

246 247

3) Weight is shifted back slightly with right toes turned out a bit, and is shifted again on to right leg, and left foot steps beside the right, toes on ground. Left hand moves in an arc before abdomen, palm up, and right hand drops with forearm before chest, palm down, forming a hold-ball gesture with the left. Then left foot takes a step forward obliquely to the left forming a left bow step, and left hand is raised before left temple, palm obliquely upward, as right hand pushes forward. Eyes on right hand. (Figs. 246, 247)

248   249   250

4) Weight is shifted on to right leg, and left toes turn in. Body turns about clockwise, and right foot is drawn beside left, toes on ground. Meanwhile, left hand drops with forearm bent horizontally, palm down, and right hand is drawn before abdomen in an arc, forming a hold-ball gesture with the left. Then body pivots about clockwise again on left toes, and right foot steps forward obliquely to the right, forming a right bow step. Meanwhile, right hand is raised before right temple, palm obliquely upward, and left hand pushes forward. Eyes on left hand. (Figs. 248 – 250)

Remember:

Hold torso erect. Do not shrug your shoulder while raising hand, and pushing out should be coordinated with bending of leg and relaxation of waist. This applies to movements on both sides. The transverse distance between heels is about 30 cm. The shuttling movements should naturally form a square diamond, facing southwest, southeast, northeast and northwest, if you start facing due south.

251   252   253

Form 55 Step Up and Grasp Peacock's Tail

1) Weight is shifted slightly back, with right toes turned out a bit, and is shifted again on to right leg. Left palm turns up and right palm turns down to form a hold-ball gesture in front of body. Meanwhile, left foot steps forward beside the right, (optionally) toes on ground. Then left foot steps forward obliquely to the left, forming a left bow step, while both hands separate. Left forearm thrusts out backhand, at shoulder level, palm in, and right hand drops beside right hip, with elbow slightly bent, palm down with fingers pointing forward. Eyes on left forearm. (figs. 251, 252)

2) Weight is shifted slightly back, and left toes turn out. Body turns left, and right foot is drawn beside the left, toes (optionally) on ground. Meanwhile, left arm is bent horizontally before chest, and right hand passes before body and goes up to the left in an arc, forming a hold-ball gesture with the left. Eyes on left hand. (Fig. 253)

The rest are the same as Form 26. (Figs. 254 − 262)

254

255

256

257

258

259

260 261 262

Form 56 Single Whip

The same as Form 4. (Figs. 263 – 267)

263   264   265

266   267

Form 57 Wave Hands Like Clouds

The same as Form 28, and the movements should be repeated five times. (Figs. 268 — 279)

268

269

270

271

272

273

274

275

276

277.

278

279

Form 58 Single Whip

The same as Form 4. (Figs. 280 – 282)

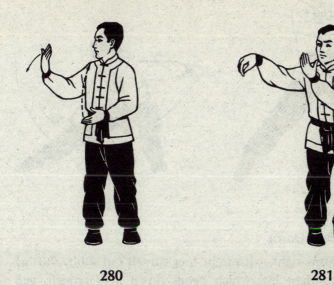

280   281

282

283   284

Form 59 Sweep Down

Torso turns right, with right toes turned out a bit, shifting weight on to right leg, which bends down in a crouch, and left heel turns outward with toes as axis, stretching left leg into a crouched side step. Meanwhile, left hand goes up to the right before right shoulder, and then sweeps down, palm outward, along the inside of left leg, and the right hook-hand is extended horizontally to the right, fingers down. Eyes on left hand. (Figs. 283 – 284)

Remember:

> In crouching, you may also turn on left toes. Both feet must rest flat on ground. Torso should not lean out too far.

285 286 287

Form 60 Golden Cock Stands on One Leg — Left and Right

1) Left toes turn out a little, and right leg gradually straightens, raising torso erect. Right toes turn in, and left leg goes on bending forward, shifting weight gradually on to left leg, and then right leg is lifted to form a one-leg stand on the left one. Meanwhile right hook-hand opens into a palm and comes to the front raised above right leg at nose level, with elbow over knee and palm facing left. Left hand drops beside left hip, palm downward. Eyes on right hand. (Figs. 285, 286)

2) Right foot drops beside (a little behind) the left with toes slightly turned out, and left leg is lifted to form a one-leg stand on the right one. Meanwhile, left hand comes up to the front to nose level, with elbow over knee and palm facing right, and right hand drops beside right hip, palm downward. Eyes on left hand. (Fig. 287)

Remember:

The single standing leg should be slightly bent. Torso must be erect and well balanced.

288   289

Form 61 Slip Back Arm — Left and Right

Torso turns slightly right, and right hand is drawn back, turning palm upward and bending elbow. As torso turns slightly left, right hand pushes forward from beside right ear, and left hand is drawn back beside left ribs, palm upward. Meanwhile, left foot takes a step backward slightly to the left, shifting weight backward, and right foot is set straight on toes, forming a hollow step. Eyes front. (Figs. 288, 289) The rest are the same as Form 17. (Figs. 290 – 295)

290 291

292 293

294

295

296 297

Form 62 Oblique Flying, Form 63 Raise Hands, Form 64 White Crane Spreading Wings, Form 65 Brush knee and Twist Step — Left, Form 66 Needle at Sea Bottom, Form 67 Flash Out Arms, Form 68 Turn, Sidle and Punch, Form 69 Step Up, Parry and Punch, Form 70 Step Up and Grasp Peacock's Tail, Form 71 Single Whip, Form 72 Wave Hands Like Moving Clouds, Form 73 Single Whip, Form 74 High Pat on Horse

Repeat movements from Figs. 81 — 135. (Figs. 296 — 349) Only movements in Form 72 Wave Hands Like Moving Clouds should be done three times, so as to return to the starting point at closing.

298 299 300

301 302

303 304 305

306 307

308

309

310

311

312

313

314

315

316

317

318 319 320

321

322

323 324 325

326

327

328

329

330

331

332

333

334 335

336 337

338

339

340

341

342   343

344   345

346

347

348

349

350

Form 75 Cross Palms (Back to Back) — Left

Right hand lowers a little, and left hand passes over back of the right and extends forward, palm obliquely upward, at eye level. Right hand goes under left elbow, palm downward. Meanwhile, left foot takes half a step forward, forming a left bow step. Eyes on left hand. (Fig. 350)

Remember:

Extending of palm and bending forward of leg should be coordinated with relaxing of waist.

351   352

Form 76 Turn, Cross Hands and Kick

Weight is shifted on to right leg, and left toes turn in. Torso turns about clockwise, shifting weight back on to left leg, and right heel is first raised off ground and then the knee. Meanwhile, hands cross in front of chest, the right before the left, palms in, and then both arms spread out, palms turned out. Right foot kicks forward. Eyes front. (Figs. 351 – 353)

Remember:

>While standing on one leg, body must be well balanced. Right leg must be kept level, and kick with the heel, straight forward.

353

354 355

Form 77 Brush Knee and Punch

Right foot is rested flat on ground with toes turned out, and body turns right. Meanwhile, right hand is lowered clenching into a fist, which is drawn beside waist with knuckles down. Left hand makes an arc upward to the right before chest, palm downward with fingers pointing backward. Then torso turns left, and left foot takes a step forward to form a left bow step. Left hand brushes over left knee, stopping beside left hip, and right fist strikes forward waist high, with knuckles facing right. Eyes front. (Figs. 354, 355)

Remember:

At completion, torso must remain erect, with waist and hips relaxed. Right arm should not be straightened.

356 357

Form 78 Step Up and Grasp Peacock's Tail

Weight is shifted slightly backward, and left toes turn out as torso turns left. Meanwhile, right fist opens into a palm drawn before abdomen, and turns upward, and left hand goes backward and up in an arc to form a hold-ball gesture with the right, while the left is on top. Meanwhile, right foot steps up beside the left, toes on ground (or not). Eyes on left hand. (Figs 356, 357) The rest are the same as Form 26. (Figs. 358 – 366)

358

359

360

361

362

363

364　　　　　　365　　　　　　366

367 368

Form 79 Single Whip

The same as Form 4. (Figs. 367 – 371)

369

370

371

372 373

Form 80 Sweep Down

The same as Form 59. (Figs. 372, 373)

374

Form 81 Step Up To Form Seven Stars

Left toes turn out slightly, and weight is shifted on to left leg gradually. Body rises erect, and right foot takes half a step forward, toes on ground, forming a right hollow step. Meanwhile, right hand also sweeps down and forward in a big arc, crossing hands with two fists before chest, back to back with the right in front. Eyes front. (Fig. 374)

Remember:

When crossing fists, the wrists must touch each other. Both arms should be rounded with muscles relaxed.

375

Form 82 Retreat To Mount Tiger

Right foot steps backward as both fists open into palms facing down and spread out, the right drawing an upward arc, stopping before right temple with palm facing obliquely out, and the left dropping before left side of waist, palm also facing obliquely out. Weight is shifted on to right leg, and left foot barely touches ground to form a left hollow step. Eyes front. (Fig. 375)

Remember:
> Finish with shoulders level and chest relaxed. Left leg is slightly bent, and both palms stretch outward with force.

376   377

Form 83 Turn and Swing Up Lotus-Leg

1) Left heel turns out with toes on ground, and right toes turn out with heel on ground. Body turns about clockwise, more than 180' left foot takes a step forward to form a left bow step. Meanwhile, left palm turns up and extends out over right wrist at eye level with fingers pointing obliquely upward, and right hand drops beneath left elbow, palm down. Eyes on left hand. (Figs. 376, 377)

378　　　　　　　　　379

2) Weight is shifted back, and body goes on turning right, with left toes turned in, shifting weight back to left leg. Then right leg is raised, and right foot swings up from left to right with leg naturally straightened. Meanwhile, right hand is raised from outside left arm, and then both hands pass over head and swing from right to left, slapping the back of right foot, left hand first, and then the right. Eyes on both hands. (Figs. 378 – 380)

Remember:

Left palm in crossing over right wrist should point at northwest. Torso leans slightly forward as right leg swings up, but keep it relaxed. It is optional whether the hands should actually touch right foot.

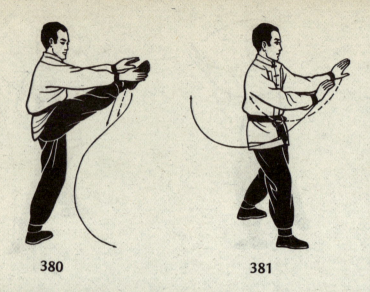

380   381

Form 84 Archer Shooting Tiger

Right foot lands in front slightly to the right, and both hands swing back, passing body, to the right, and turn into fists. Right fist comes up and forward beside right temple with knuckles facing head, and left fist passes before face and extends forward to the left, knuckles facing obliquely backward, nose high. Meanwhile, right leg bends to form a right bow leg. Eyes on left fist. (Figs. 381 – 383)

Remember:

When both hands swing back, torso and head should turn in the same direction. Eyes are first to the right, and then turn on left fist. At completion, body must be erect, and both arms are rounded. If you start facing south, the bow step goes southeast, and left fist thrusts toward northeast.

382

383

384 385

Form 85 Step Up, Parry and Punch

1) Right toes turn in, and body turns left, shifting weight on to left leg. Left toes turn out, and then right foot is drawn beside the left. Meanwhile, right fist swings down left, stopping before left ribs, knuckles up, and left fist opens into a palm, facing upward, and is drawn back, making an arc on left side with palm turned down before chest. (Figs. 384, 385)

2) The rest are the same as in Figs. 47 – 49. (Figs. 386 – 388)

 386

 387

 388

Form 86 Apparent Close and Form 87 Cross Hands

The same as in Figs. 50 — 57. (Figs. 389 — 396)

389

390

391

392

393   394

395

396 397

Form 88 Closing Form

Both palms turn out, spreading downward and gradually rest on the outside of both legs. The whole body relaxes with eyes looking straight forward. Then left foot moves beside the right to a standstill. (Figs. 397 – 400)

Remember:
> When both hands go down, breathe slowly. Draw back left foot when breath is normal again. On closing, take a slow walk, and do not get into vigorous action immediately.

398

399

400

III. The Diagram of Footwork for Taijiquan (88-Forms)

1. The whole series in fact moves many times back and forth along a straight line, which can only be indicated by projection as above.

2. The forms that remain on the same spot are grouped close to each other.

3. The top of the form number represents the back of the practitioner, whereas the bottom his front.

4. The whole series comprises 88 forms, some of which are repeated more than once, such as, "Slip Back Forearm", "Wave Hands Like Moving Clouds", "Parting Wild Horse's Mane" etc. These are shown with repetitions separately indicated.
   To return to where the exercise begins, the practitioner may choose to repeat "Wave Hands Like Moving Clouds" either twice or four times in doing the form. Generally, Form 28 is repeated four times, Form 57 four times and Form 72 twice.

5. The practitioner is supposed to start facing south. Throughout the descriptions, his face is facing the front, his back the rear, his left hand the left and right hand the right. If a form finishes in an oblique direction, then it is indicated as 45' SE of 45' NW etc.

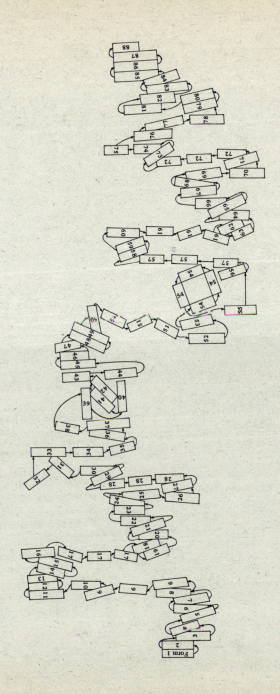

Chapter Three

THE TAIJI PUSH-HANDS

This is a dual exercise of Taijiquan rather like a contest. There are two forms: stationary and mobile. The exercise, combined with the solo, can help improve the practitioners' technique in Taijiquan as well as their agility and response through mutual cooperation. Beginners may also practise the dual exercise along with the solo to cultivate their art in both. The aim of the exercise is health preservation rather than physical contest.

The beginner should start with single-hand practice, and go on to the dual stationary and mobile push-hands. He should proceed from the simple to the more evolved forms, and not expect to jump at quick success without a solid foundation, While in practice, the movements must run on smoothly with flexibility, and the arms should never be held rigid. The partners should neither break off nor clash with each other, but are all along, as it were, stuck together.

Note:
1) To make the positions and directions of movement clear and definite, the partners' positons are never changed in the pictures (except in mobile forms).
2) All the movements of Partner A are indicated by dotted lines, of B by single lines.
3) In practising the mobile form, the beginners should master one side of it before going on to the other side. After a certain period, the partners will naturally be "stuck together" without break, whether going forward or backward, at will.

I. Basic Training

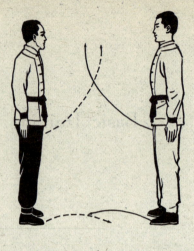

1

I. Pre-Opening Stance

The two partners stand erect face to face, fully relaxed. Their distance is kept at two arms' length, with their fists barely able to touch each other. (Fig. 1)

2

The start: Both turn half left, taking a step forward with right foot so that the insides of the feet face each other about 10 — 20) cm apart. Both raise right arms, slightly bent, and cross their right wrists, back to back, (called "contact") while their left hands hang down naturally and their weights rest on both legs. (Fig. 2)

Remember:
Their arms should be slightly strained at contact, which is neither too hard nor too soft.

3

II. Single Hand Practice

1) A turns right palm towards B, pushing his wrist back, bends right leg to shift weight forward slightly, and bears down upon the right of B's chest with right hand. (Fig. 3)

B meet A's challenge with strength, neither softly nor hard, withdraws right hand, and bends left leg slightly to shift weight backward. He then turns torso right and parries A's right hand with his own right palm, to keep body intact. (Fig. 4)

2) As A's right hand is deflected, B immediately pushes forward with right palm at A's wrist, bearing down towards the right of A's chest. (Fig. 5)

4

5

6

A meets B's challenge the same way. He withdraws right arm, bends left leg to shift weight back, and turns torso to parry B's right palm. (Fig. 6) The partners go on by turns; the movement of their hands keep making a horizontal circle.

> Note: When A pushes towards B, B should deflect the impact by turning his waist. Conversely, when B pushes towards A, A should also deflect the impact by turning his waist.

Remember:
> In pushing forward, the torso should not lean out too far; in deflecting, turn at waist with hips drawn in, but never lean back while weight is shifted backward. The arms of both partners should always remain a bit strained, and are alternately bent or extended. Their contact is neither soft nor hard, and without brake, as if their wrists were stuck together or spun around each other like a bearing around a shaft. Meanwhile, their left hands should remain flexible to help keep balance.

7

3) Both partners start over again, as in Fig. 2. But A turns right palm forward and upward as it pushes B's wrist, aiming at his face, and bends forward right leg to shift weight forward. B strains right arm and raises it on A's strength, but bends left leg slightly backward to shift weight back. He turns torso right and deflects A's right palm away from right temple. (Fig. 7)

8

4) B smoothly turns right palm down and pushes forward towards A's right ribs; A in turn meets B's challenge with right hand, and withdraws it on B's strength. Meanwhile, he bends left leg and turns torso right to shift weight back, deflecting B's right hand to the right. (Figs. 8, 9)

5) When A's right hand pushes towards B's face, B turns torso slightly right, and parries with right hand to deflect A's right hand from right temple, and immediately pushes towards A's face. A turns right to deflect B's right arm and turns palm forward and down towards B's right ribs. (Fig. 10 – 12)

These movements can go on and on, with the hands moving in vertical circles. From time to time, the two partners may change their steps and hands from right to left.

9

10

11

12

13

III. Horizontal Milling with Both Hands

1) Following "contact" with right hands, each puts his left palm on the other's right elbow. (Fig. 13)

14

2) A turns right palm to B and presses B's right wrist back and down, while his left hand pushes B's right elbow in the same direction trying to force B's right arm inert against chest. (This is called "press") (Fig. 14 – 15)

B's right arm meets A's push with some strength, but his left hand on A's right elbow gradually draws it out, and his left leg bends slightly to shift weight back. With his chest drawn in a little, he turns body right, and deflects A's push to the right, off its mark. (This is called "deflection".) (Fig. 16)

3) Following the deflection, B immediately turns right palm and puts it on A's right wrist. Then he pushes out and down with both hands just as A did to him. (Figs. 17, 18) A deflects B's pressing just as B did to him. (ref. Figs. 13 – 18) This can go on as long as desired.

15

16

17

18

II. Stationary Push-Hands

        19   20

The opening stance is the same as in Fig. 2.

1) *Fending:* A and B make contact, both with right hand slightly strained. (Fig. 19)

2) *Shunting:* A turns right palm to B's right wrist and draws backward while putting left hand on B's right elbow. Taking advantage of B's challenge, he bends left leg, draws in hip and turns right at waist. With both hands on B's right arm, he shunts it to the right. (Fig. 20)

21   22

3) *Pushing:* As A draws back and turns, B bends forward right leg slightly, shifting weight forward a little. Meanwhile, with his left palm on the inside of right arm, he pushes forward with right forearm towards A's chest to foil A's shunting and force both his hands inert against chest. (Fig. 21)

4) *Pressing:* On the strength of B's push, A bends left leg, draws in chest and turns left at waist, with hip drawn in. Meanwhile both his hands press B's right arm down to the left to deflect it. Then A's right hand is immediately turned upon B's left elbow, and his left hand is shifted to B's left wrist. Both hands press forward with palms downward. (Fig. 22)

23 24

5) B meets A's pressing with strength. As he turns the back of left hand towards A's left palm, his right hand comes up from the right and rests on A's left elbow. Meanwhile, he bends left leg, shifting weight back, and turns left. With his left arm against A's pressing (and not withdrawing), both his hands go up left to shunt aside A's left arm. (Fig. 23)

6) At B's shunting, A detaches right hand from B's left elbow, and immediately puts it on the inside of his own left elbow in order to keep his balance. He rounds both arms and pushes out towards B's chest. (Figs. 24. 25)

7) On the strength of A's push, B draws in chest, turns at waist, drawing back hips, and begins pressing. (Figs. 26, 27)

8) As B presses forward, A stops him with right arm, and raises left hand to put it on B's right elbow, with his body turned right. So now A is in a shunting position with B pushing. (Fig. 28)

25 26

27 28

29   **30**

9) *Change hands:* As B pushes towards A's chest, (ref. Fig. 21), A does not go into a pressing position, but takes B's left hand with his own left and shunts B's left elbow with his right. He turns left slightly and changes into shunting aside B's left arm. (Fig. 29)

When B's left arm is shunted aside by A, B should quickly change into pushing with left arm, with right leg still bent forward. (Fig. 30) When A has deflected B's push and begun pressing, B's left arm should come up from left side and rest upon A's right elbow. He sits back to shunt aside A's right arm, and A instantly changes into pressing. (Fig. 31)

The formula is: A shunting — B pushing; B pushing — A pressing; A pressing — B fending; Then B turns into shunting — A into pressing; A shunting — B turns into pressing; B pressing — A fending, and turns into shunting. This can repeat many times.

31

III. Mobile Push-Hands

32

I. 3 Steps Forward, 2 Backward

The opening stance is almost the same as that of Stationary Push-Hands, only at contact, A puts his left foot forward while B his right, with B's right outside A's left, both in a walking stance. They cross their left hands, and put their right on each other's left elbow. A is pushing with left arm, while B is ready to press. (Fig. 32)

33

1) B moves a step with right foot to put it inside A's left while his hands press A's right arm. (Fig. 33)

2) A steps back with left foot, and his right hand takes B's right over his own left elbow. Meanwhile, his left hand moves around on the left and rests on B's right elbow, ready for shunting. Following A's shunting, B takes another (the second) step forward with left foot outside A's right, to prepare for pushing. (Fig. 34)

3) A retreats one more (the second) step with right foot, while his hands shunt B's right arm to the right, and his body turns naturally in the act. Following A's shunting, B takes still another (the third) step forward with right foot inside A's left, and bends forward right leg, with both arms still pushing out. A slightly bends right leg, shifting weight backward and drawing hips into begin pressing. (Figs. 35, 36)

34

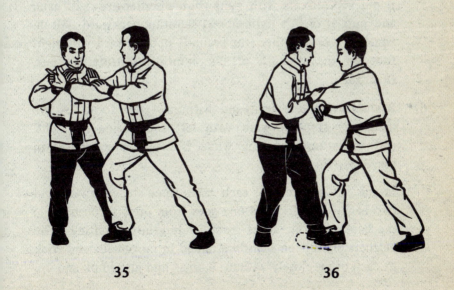

35 36

37

4) Taking advantage of B's push A turns slightly left at the waist while shifting left foot inside B's right (A's first step forward), and his hands press forward. (Fig. 37)

5) B quickly retreats with right foot, disentangles right hand and puts it on A's right elbow, shunting backward. Meanwhile A takes another (the second) step forward with right foot on the strength of B's shunting, outside B's left. (Fig. 38)

6) B shunts A's left arm, and withdraws left foot. A immediately steps forward with left foot inside B's right, and turns into pushing while B begins pressing (as in Fig. 32). (Fig. 39)

In this set of exercise, each takes three steps forward and two back. The forward one goes from press to push while the backward one turns from fending into shunting. The partners should be slightly strained in movement and stick to each other closely without a break and just go on and on.

38

39

40 41

II. 3 steps Forward, 3 Backward

The opening stance is just the same as that of Stationary Push-hands. The process is almost the same as the former set (3 forward, 2 backward), only there is one more step backward in movement, and both begin with right foot forward.

The footwork: On contact, the forward one advances one step with right foot while the backward one retreats one step with his left to make room for the three steps forward and three backward.

1) Both put their right foot forward. A pushes with left arm toward B's chest, his right hand on the inside of left elbow in support and right leg bent forward. B draws in hips and chest to start pressing while shifting right foot forward a bit, and A retreats a step with the left (both the first step). Then B advances again with left foot while A retreats with the right (the second step). Their arm movements are the same as in the former set. After that, B advances again with right foot, and A retreats again with his left (the third step). In short, the whole process is:

42

A goes from pushing, through fending and shunting, into pressing, while B's arms turn from pressing into pushing. (Figs. 40 — 44)

43

44

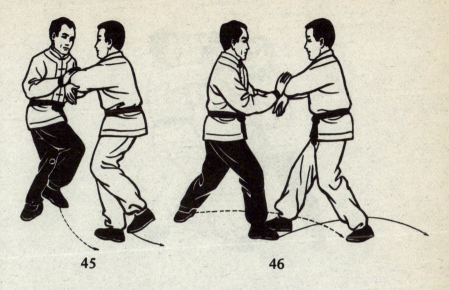

45   46

2) A advances and B retreats just as they did in opposite roles, only A steps forward with right foot while B retreats first with the left. (Figs. 45 – 48)

47

48

49   50

III. Mobile shunting

The Pre-opening and Opening Stances are the same as in Figs. 1, 2. (Fig. 49)

1) A turns right palm to take, very lightly, B's right wrist, and puts left wrist on B's right elbow. Meanwhile, his left heel turns outward on toes, and right foot takes half a step back beside the left, with body turned half right to begin shunting. Following closely, B takes half a step forward to put left foot beside the right, shifting weight forward a little. (Fig. 50)

Another way is: B takes half a step forward with right foot as A begins shunting.

51   52

2) With this, A turns body right and backward, retreating a step with right foot. Meanwhile, his hands shunt B's right arm sideways to draw him out. B has to take a long step forward with left foot, and his body leans out almost off balance. (Fig. 51)

3) As A goes on shunting, B steps forward again with right foot inside A's left, shifting weight slightly forward onto right leg. Meanwhile, his left hand is on the inside of right arm, and his shoulder leans against A's chest. (Fig. 52)

53

4) A meets B's impact by swinging left elbow out and turning body slightly right to defect it. Then he draws in chest and turns left at waist to shift weight on to right leg, while his hand change from shunting into pressing (left hand pressing B's left down, and right hand pressing B's left elbow), and his left foot takes a quick step forward inside B's right. (Fig. 53)

54

5) Following A's pressing, B meets A's left hand with the back of his own left, and disentangles his right hand from under the left to put it on A's left elbow. Meanwhile, his right foot retreats half a step beside the left, and his body turns left slightly, changing the leaning position into shunting. But A's right foot remains forward, and his left leg bends forward slightly, shifting weight a bit to the front. (Fig. 54)

6) B turns body left while his left foot takes a step backward obliquely to the left; his hands remain shunting (the left against A's left wrist, and right wrist against A's left elbow). At this A takes a long step forward with right foot, shifting weight slightly forward on to right leg. (Fig. 55)

7) A's left foot steps forward again inside B's right, shifting weight forward on to left leg. Meanwhile, he puts right hand on the inside of left arm in support, and leans against B's chest with shoulder. (Fig. 56)

55

56

57

As above, A and B take turns to advance or retreat, each time being a round. Or, B may cut forward with right foot to start pressing, while A retreats to change into shunting. (Figs. 57, 58) This can go on, round after round, as long as desired.

The change of hands in Mobile shunting: To get out of a defensive position, A deflects B's leaning shoulder by turning left elbow clockwise, while his right hand quickly claws at B's face (called Lightning palm). At this, B should raise right hand to meet A's right and take it by the wrist, and his left wrist is laid on A's right elbow. Meanwhile, he turns right, drawing his right foot beside the left, and begins shunting with both hands. As A is shunted by B, he takes a step forward with right foot, shifting weight forward, and stops in front of B's feet. (Figs. 59 – 61)

58   59

60   61

      62   63

8)   B smoothly turns right, and steps backward with right foot while his hands go on shunting. Drawn out by B, A takes a big step forward with left foot, shifting weight forward, and his right goes on another step, stopping inside B's left foot. Meanwhile, his left hand is on the inside of right elbow as both arms push towards B's chest. (Fig. 62)

The process is similar to the former set of Mobile shunting, only in the former, A shunts B's right arm while B shunts A's left arm, and the partners change roles by one taking a quick step, turning shunting into pressing to deflect the other's impact. In the latter, each shunts the other's right arm, and changes role by clawing with right hand.

If B claws at A's face with left hand, A should take B's left arm with left hand, and turn left to begin shunting. Meanwhile, B advances with left arm against A's chest. Then the two can go on clawing with left hand, and are shunted off by the left arm. (Figs. 63 — 66)

64

65

66